LIVING IN
THE LIGHT

LIVING IN THE LIGHT

Sunny Buchanan
Who Listened to the Light
Within for Guidance

Alice Naomi Sweet

Library of Congress Control Number:		2004090970
ISBN 10:	Hardcover	1-4134-4735-X
	Softcover	1-4134-4734-1
ISBN 13:	Hardcover	978-1-4134-4735-4
	Softcover	978-1-4134-4734-7

Photographs were taken by Dawn Greene, Gladys Myers, and Cody Sweet.

This book was printed in the United States of America.

To order additional copies of this book, contact:
Xlibris Corporation
1-888-795-4274
www.Xlibris.com
Orders@Xlibris.com
22917

To readers who appreciate the goodness which promotes progress and light.

Butterflies brighten the flowers,
bless the soul,
and beautify the earth.
May sunny days be ahead.

PREFACE

In 1964 I attended a Wednesday night testimony meeting at a Wilmette, Illinois church. The parishioners were all white except one. This lady stood up and gave a testimony about the good that God brought into her life. After the meeting I thanked her for her testimony. We became friends. This book is based on her life.

Some people knew her as Ammie. I knew her as Sunny because she spread sunshine into many of the things she said and did.

CONTENTS

CHAPTER ONE

THE SUNSHINE OF GOOD

"There is no wealth, but life."
John Ruskin

"When a man is happy he does not hear the clock strike."
John Ruskin

"Happiness makes up in height for what it lacks in length."
Robert Frost

The Early Morning sunbeams blessed the cotton fields with warmth. Big Ma worked in the field, and her bag was almost filled with white cotton balls. As she picked the soft balls, she thanked God for governing the world including the cotton fields. Big Ma recalled, during her childhood, attending a Methodist camp meeting. She heard that in the Saxon and twenty other languages, *good* is the term for God. Down through the ages one letter o was dropped. Learning that about the word *God* as coming from the word *good* is when she got religion. She really did get religion. Big Ma, with her rich, clear voice, was often humming praises to God for the limited view of the world she knew in the late 1880's.

Big Ma was a sensible, pious woman. She was hard working and a person to be trusted. Her black hair, fine as floss silk, hung around her dimpled face. Her faith-filled eyes, full of love and softness, sparkled under her blue sunbonnet. She thanked *Good* for her endurance to work in the bountiful cotton fields. She wondered what Good had in store for her today. Big Ma expected good to happen to everyone. Her sturdy, wide, solid body suddenly straightened to her almost six feet. An unseen force was telling her that Em's baby was coming. She needed to be there to deliver that baby. She said to herself, "Something good is coming today—Em's baby."

Big Ma's bare feet flew through the tall grass and carried her home. She hitched her beloved horse, Old Bill, to a small cart. With soft words she urged Old Bill on to her daughter Em's home.

Big Ma's daughter, Em, lived in a plank house in the east pasture of the old King plantation. Em's house, on stilts, half-hidden in the tall grass, had no windows. It just had a front and back door. The house was one big room with a wood stove centered on one wall, with a table and chairs in the front, and bunks along both sides in back to sleep on.

Big Ma could hardly hear Em's cries because the rooster was crowing so loudly as it strutted underneath the house awakening the turkeys, geese, chickens, ducks, guinea fowl, hogs, sheep and goats. The animals all shared the protection of the house with the dogs and cats. Em was alone on a quilt on the wood floor. Em's husband, Levy, had gone for Em's sister, Maggie. They weren't back yet.

Big Ma grumbled, "Always said Maggie would be late for her own funeral. Takes her so long to wash her feet before she goes any place." Big Ma looked closely at Em and said, "Now this babe's going to be here before Maggie is! The lamp has most burnt out all the kerosene. I'll fix that."

Big Ma wiped Em with a cold cloth and sang to her amid the screams. Between screams and hallelujahs the baby girl was born. A burst of sunlight came in through the doorway and illuminated the room.

Big Ma and her daughter hadn't thought of a name for the baby. Big Ma said, "Let's name her Sunny for the sunshine."

Levy and Maggie showed up after the delivery was complete.

SOAP MAKING

When Big Ma did the washing, she said, "I can't find no soap, only this little piece. This all the soap you have?"

Em told her, "I was going to make soap, but the babe came sooner than I expected. See, there are plenty of hog bones."

Big Ma went out on the gallery, the porch. She looked at the scraggly pine trees around the house and said to Levy, "I'm going to make some white soap for this gorgeous babe. Don't want no hickory wood. Don't want no red soap. This first babe is going to have white soap."

Big Ma said to Levy, "You go to the hills and fetch me some cedar wood."

Levy was glad for an excuse to get away from the women. He didn't even look at Em or the babe. He took a huge hunk of cornpone, grabbed his axe, and took off for the hills. Big Ma made Em take some Ripple Soup. She always made Ripple Soup when anyone was under the weather. The ripples are made with eggs, flour, butter, seasoned a bit, stirred together and poured by teaspoons into hot milk.

Big Ma was a singer. She was singing now, "When we all git to Heaven, what a joyful day that will be. When we all see Jesus, we will sing and shout for jubilee."

Big Ma crossed the dark room singing as she moved outside into the gallery. There in the hot May sunshine, Big Ma was happy to be doing good for someone.

She cleaned out a three legged, iron, black pot hanging on a rod between two iron posts. Then she turned to a contraption that looked like a wheelbarrow on stilts. It was an ashhopper. She readied it for Levy's return with some cedar wood.

When Levy brought the cedar wood, Big Ma took the wood and burned it. She culled through the ashes, making sure there was no mixed wood in the ashes. Then she placed the ashes in the ashhopper. She poured water over the ashes and let it drip. Liquid poured out like wine into the tub under the hopper. Big Ma taught Em never to throw anything away. "Anything can be used for something." She threw the hog bones into the three legged pot along with the leftovers of the meat—pork bones and skin. She poured the ash water over the bones and skins and sprinkled crystals of lye on top of the mixture. The mixture was boiled until all the bones, fat meat, and skins disappeared. Any pieces that did not dissolve were lifted out with a wooden spoon. Soap has three simple ingredients—*fat, lye, and water.*

Big Ma stirred the mixture and checked about every twenty minutes to see if the soap was done. It was done when it left a creamy layer on the spoon. While the water boiled, Big Ma skimmed off the grease about four inches deep into the galvanized tub. This tub was often used for washing clothes and bathing. She also used whatever cans and buckets she could find.

The grease was the soap. The soap didn't get hard immediately. You could use it, but it was better to wait. The next morning Big Ma turned the tub and cans upside down, knocked the soap out, and cut it up into bar sized pieces. She left the bars of soap outside on a board to continue drying.

In a few days the soap was ready to use. She stored the soap in a cardboard box. Home made soap is used for getting spots out of clothing. Just dampen the spot, rub it with soap, then wash the garment along with the other clothes.

Big Ma told Maggie, "Don't you put too much soap in the water for the babe. Don't let none git in her eyes! You hear? It's too strong." Big Ma told Maggie to take some soap home with her and to see that Levy takes some to his mama. Levy's mama was a Black Creek Indian.

Big Ma would say, "Levy's mama was one of the ugliest women you ever saw, but was she smart." Her hair, coarse as a mule's tail, hung down to her waist. Levy's daddy was mostly Greek. Levy was called a half-breed. He had straight, coal black hair. He was short, strong as an ox with not an inch of fat on him. Levy was a drinker. He loved his whiskey.

So on May 8, 1887, in Yazoo, Mississippi, Sunny King was born in a one room, wooden house in the valley of the old King plantation. Sunny was born midst joyful singing and thankfulness to God. Sunny was delivered by her own grandmother, Big Ma.

CHAPTER TWO

DEEP SOUTH

"Wherever there is a human being,
there is an opportunity for kindness."
Seneca

"And he spoke a parable unto them to this end,
that men ought always to pray."
Luke 18:1 (KJV)

"Men are made for happiness and anyone who is
completely happy has a right to say to himself:
I am doing God's work on earth."
Anthon Chekhov

Big Ma's Mother, Sunny's great grandma, was born a slave. Big Ma, Sunny's grandmother, was a former slave, too. Em was Sunny's mother. Em was the first person in the family to be born free.

Em never knew her birth date. She only knew that she was six weeks old the Christmas of the South's surrender in the Civil War. When Em's mother, Big Ma, was a child, she was put on a block and sold along with her mother and sisters, Lucindie, Ramissa, Ayo, Effie and her grandmother. The family was all separated. When they were sold, they were given new names by the people who bought them. After the South's surrender, they found each other and had a reunion. They knew they belonged together because their hands were alike. Their hands were short, stubby and big at the ends. Their feet were alike. The toe next to the big toe was short.

Em was a quiet, sober child. She liked to sit in the swing under the pecan tree and watch her sister, Maggie, and friends play tag, hide and seek, and jump rope. While they laughed and chattered, Em was content to observe. Big Ma taught her daughter early in life that there was not any sense in complaining. Em went with Big Ma to church, but she never understood what going to church was about. Often when sent to attend first grade in school, Em would hide under the cobshed until school was over. She never attended much afterwards. Em never learned to read and write. She always signed her name with an x. Em used bad language toward almost everyone. She was jealous of her older brother. He was successful in what he did. Em never had a good word to say about him.

Big Ma would say to Em,

> There was a little girl, who had a little curl
> Right in the middle of her forehead
> When she was good
> She was very, very good
> When she was bad, she was horrid.

Then Big Ma would say, "Em, I see worms, spiders, snakes, flies, wasps, hornets coming out of your mouth."

That would quiet Em. She was moody and critical until the day she died. Her sister, Maggie, was the opposite. She was full of laughter and participated joyously in school activities.

When a man named Levy came into Em's life, she sparkled. She loved Levy. They had a church wedding. Almost everyone in the valley came. After they were married, they liked to dance under the stars out on the gallery. Levy sang love songs in his rich baritone voice. Later they were happy playing with their baby, Sunny.

When Sunny was three months old, Em tripped. Sunny was dropped on a red hot stove by accident. It got so hot in Mississippi that when you were cooking, the stovetop turned red. Levy, crying all the way, went for Big Ma. There were no doctors. Sometimes a traveling doctor, dentist, or man selling eyeglasses would come through. When Big Ma took the baby in her arms, the crying ceased. Big Ma sat in the rocking chair with the baby in her arms all day, all night, and all the next day. She prayed trusting God to heal Sunny. Big Ma could see some wounds healing before her eyes. There would remain a big scar on Sunny's left arm. Big Ma was telling folks how courageous Sunny was when the left side of her body was burned. She didn't cry out and fuss. Her arm was still disfigured when she went to school. She'd say to her schoolmates, "That's the reward I got for falling on a red hot stove." The scar grew dimmer through the years until you could barely see it. Big Ma said, "Sunny is no complainer. This scar is Sunny's badge of honor for bravery."

When Sunny was about eighteen months old, her daddy's brothers, Willie, Joe, and Lem came to visit. Her daddy went hunting for deer and bear in the swamps with them. Her daddy and his brothers never came back. Em sat on the gallery steps staring off at the path toward the swamp day after day expecting Levy to return. Methodically Em cared for Sunny. The whole valley mourned. Searching parties went into the swamps, but no trace was ever found of the men. It was speculated that a bear got them, or more likely, while trying to help each other, they died in the quicksand that was hidden from view in the swamps. Big Ma arrived one day in her buggy and took Em and Sunny home with her.

HAPPY CHILDHOOD

Em and her daughter were happy living with Big Ma. There were beds of flowers around the home. The flowers had every color of the rainbow and different names. Em would pick nasturtiums, sit in the rocking chair under the pecan tree, and be very quiet. Sometimes she moaned and wiped her eyes. Em told Sunny that nasturtiums were Levy's favorite flower. When Em was married at the church, Levy had given her a bunch of nasturtiums.

Sunny's earliest recollection was running after a wagon drawn by mules going by her home and calling "Daddy, Daddy!" The wagon didn't stop. Sunny turned and saw her Mama standing in the doorway crying. Sunny was sad and cried.

On Sunday afternoons until after twilight, Big Ma sat in her rocking chair under the pecan tree singing songs of thanks to Good. When the fireflies and mosquitoes came out, she came in the house and lit the kerosene lamp.

When Sunny was four years old, she went with Big Ma to a picnic in a neighbor's back yard. The neighbor's boys were playing in their treehouse. Sunny climbed up the steps nailed into the trunk of the tree until she had her head through the trap door. The boys were trying to lift her into the treehouse and pushed the trapdoor the wrong way so that her air supply was cut off. When they got her down, Sunny was unconscious. Big Ma kept screaming, "Oh, they killed my baby!" Sunny was placed under the pump in the back yard. Cold water and Big Ma's prayers brought her back to consciousness.

When the cherries were ripe, Sunny climbed and sat high in the bountiful Cherry tree. As she picked she sang "Cherries are ripe, Cherries are ripe, The Robin sang one day, Cherries are ripe, Will you come out and play?" The song was in the *McGuffey Reader* her teacher had at school.

Em made cherry pie. When the peaches were ripe, Em made peach cobbler. Big Ma always made the apple dumplings. Everyone said Big Ma made the best chicken and dumplings in the valley.

CORNCOB DOLLS

The only dolls Sunny had were corncob dolls. They were made from dried out corncobs. The dolls were easy to make. Corncobs were plentiful. If a doll got lost or dirty, it was easily replaced.

Sunny liked to play school with her dolls. She had the corncob dolls in all heights. The tallest and widest was the teacher. She lined the dolls up by size from first grade through eighth. If one of her dolls misbehaved while she was telling them one of the stories her teacher told at school, she put the doll in the corner.

At Christmas and on Sunny's birthday, Sunny's mama, Em, made Sunny a beautiful corncob doll. Em had a gift for sewing. Sunny took special care of the dolls Em made. Sunny gave them special names. Her favorite name for a boy doll was Sky. For a girl it was Princess or Angel.

All you do to make a corncob doll is to take a dry corncob being sure all the kernels have been removed. Then you paint a face on the corncob. Draw eyes, nose and mouth on the top part of the corncob. If you wanted to make a red mouth, you made red ink from a mixture of water and soot from the stove. For the hair, a handful of dry cornsilk was placed across the top of the corncob, centering it so that it hung down equally on two sides like pigtails. For clothing, scraps of cloth were wrapped around the corncob.

A NEIGHBOR THEY CALLED GRANDPA

Sunny liked to walk down the dusty road and visit Grandpa Davis. Big Ma sent him hot biscuits, pies or whatever special she was baking. Trees with beds of Lillies of the Valley surrounded his home. Sunny liked to pick bouquets of them for Big Ma. It was a family joke that you were going to have flowers for dinner. Big Ma put the flowers and plates on before she fixed the food.

Grandpa Davis lived alone. No longer did he look like the huge, muscular, six foot four black soldier who marched with General Sherman to the sea. He was bent over, had trouble walking and trouble doing the small chores around his home. Sunny helped him. She washed his dishes and cleaned his home. Big Ma did his washing and ironing. They received no pay. Colored folks just took care of each other.

Grandpa said, "Sunny, I deserve the bad things that happened to me. I can't forget the sorrow on the faces of the old folks, women, and children when I marched with General Sherman.

Their men were in the Confederate army. I joined the volunteers of Germans, Irish, Scotch, English, and Negroes in Chattanooga. We were lean, mean, and strong. I fought in the Battle of Bull Run and the Battle of Shiloh. We were fighting against a real army then. I never felt badly about that."

When Grandpa Davis told stories about the march with General Sherman, he'd cry. Then Sunny would cry. He told Sunny that General Tecumseh Sherman was from Ohio. He was educated at the United States Military Academy and became a Union General in the Civil War.

He sorrowfully told Sunny, "We left Atlanta in flames. There were about 62,000 men. Most of us were on foot. We had around 5,000 cavalry horses and about 2,000 riding artillery horses. Our army fanned out in about a sixty mile span from one side to the other. We destroyed the land, homes, people, bridges, railroads— anything that was in our way we burned and destroyed."

Grandpa Davis read to Sunny what General Sherman said, "War is hell. There is many a boy here who looks on war as all glory, but, boys, it is all hell. You can bear this warning voice to generations to come." Grandpa Davis agreed, "War is hell." Sunny got to hear all this information from a person who experienced it.

The United States government gave Grandpa a Civil War pension. He married a lovely red-haired girl and had nine children. A handsome, singing, fiddle playing, dancing salesman came to the valley. He had pots, pans, jewelry, tools, clothing, medicine and most anything you could think of. Most traveling salesmen and preachers stayed a few days. This one stayed three weeks. No one knew when he left, but he left during the night with Grandpa's wife and all nine children. They went to Memphis. Over the years Grandpa's daughter, Bell, came back occasionally to visit her dad. Sunny called her Aunt Bell.

Aunt Bell had flaming red hair like her mother. She married a wealthy Memphis business man. They had no children. She liked Sunny and brought her material for Em to make her dresses. Aunt Bell brought Sunny candy, shoes, and a beautiful cameo ring. It was a happy time for Sunny when Aunt Bell came to visit.

Sunny remembered another traveling salesman who came to the valley selling eyeglasses. Grandpa, the salesman, and Sunny were standing on the gallery on the front of Grandpa's home overlooking the trees and beds of Lillies of the Valley.

The salesman took Grandpa's glasses off his nose and said, "No wonder you're having trouble seeing. These glasses are no good. You need new glasses. You'll be able to read clearly with the glasses I have."

The salesman raised his arm and threw Grandpa's old glasses out among the grass and Lillies of the Valley. The salesman left town the same day. Grandpa couldn't see out of the new glasses as well as the old glasses. Sunny spent an hour searching for his old glasses. She didn't find them. Grandpa told Sunny, "That man is a snake. He just pretended to throw my old glasses away. He kept them to sell to someone else."

SHADOWS CLOUDING SUNLIGHT

A large soft-shell pecan tree grew in the meadow. The pecans were over an inch long. Big Ma made rolls with pecans, pies with pecans, and delicious pecan candy. One day a crew of surveyors and workmen came by. They told Big Ma a highway was going to run through the meadow. The pecan tree had to come down. The pecan tree was like an old friend to Big Ma. She begged the men to spare her tree. With Big Ma, Em, Sunny, and the neighbors standing around crying, workmen cut down the huge tree. Big Ma moaned and cried for her tree for years after it was cut down. She never understood how the government could come in and do what they wanted with your property. The tree was gone, but they never did build that highway.

FARMING COTTON

Big Ma farmed cotton. She had thirty acres. Big Ma worked the land called **"halfers-hands."** The white man took **half** of what she made because he owned the land. If she didn't make a substantial amount, then he took whatever she had. Big Ma had to make enough money from the cotton to pay the white owner and have enough to live on until the next crop.

It took Big Ma several weeks to plow the soil. Then she had to wait until the soil was warm enough before planting the cottonseeds. If the soil is too cold, the cottonseeds will not grow. In about ten days, the seedlings appear above the soil. It takes about five weeks more for small flower buds to form. The buds expand and become white flowers.

When the white flowers fall off, a fluffy white **boll** grows right where the flower was. In about 180 days from the time the cottonseeds were planted, the boll bursts open to show the fiber inside. The cotton is ready to harvest.

Cotton was worth 5 1/2 cents a pound. Sometimes it would take more than two bales of cotton to pay for the rental of the land. Sometimes Big Ma made five bales in all. Bales weighed 450 to 500 pounds. Big Ma took the bales to the mill and had it ginned to take out the seeds. She would sell it for 25 cents or 30 cents a pound or maybe not that much.

Staple is the fiber of cotton. The price of cotton depended on what grade staple the cotton was. Staple is graded as to length and fineness capable of being spun into yarn. The value of the cotton depended on whether it was long staple or short staple. Big Ma got more for the long staple. Big Ma made enough money to carry her and her family from one season to the next.

Sunny began working in the cotton fields when she was eight years old. She liked working in the cotton fields. She wasn't strong enough to pull a bag of cotton, so she worked on the same row as Big Ma and put the cotton in her bag. Sunny chopped cotton as well as picked cotton. Chopping cotton is when you hoe to thin it out. Sunny was Big Ma's plow boy.

HAPPINESS

Big Ma grew her own food. She canned her own garden vegetables and had her own horses, cows, and sheep. There was plenty of food. There were no stores. There was only the commissary and that was miles away. Sunny's Grandma killed and cured her own meat, smoked her own bacon, ham, sides, middlins. She raised everything except flour. She grew black eyed peas, too. That's white peas with a little black speck on them. She also had shinnie peas. Shinney peas were a brown pea with specks. Then she raised clay peas. That's a solid brown pea. Big Ma grew pole beans, snap beans, butter beans, okra, spinach, kohlrabi, head lettuce, leaf lettuce, bibs lettuce, squash, turnip greens, mustard greens, rutabeggers, cabbage, rice, sweet and Irish tatters. The best yams were the white poplars. The hull was red and the insides white. Just as sweet as a tatter could be.

Big Ma grew her own grubbers. They are what you call peanuts. She grew them along with the squash and melons. Dark folks like salt pork washed and cooked in a pot. Then it's smothered with mustard greens and cabbage greens and cooked until tender. Big Ma said, "People who fry up their food don't know what they is missing. It's the broth that's good. It's the whole soul food of vegetables and things cooked up like that."

While the folks worked hard, they had good times too. The folks in the valley enjoyed fishing. A happy day for Sunny and Big Ma was to hitch up Old Bill, take fried chicken and fresh biscuits with fried apples, and drive down the road to Blueberry Creek. Big Ma liked to fish by the bridge. They used poles with string and hooks. They dug their own worms for bait from the soft earth in the garden. Big Ma told Sunny stories while they fished. They sang old gospel songs. The clean, caressing odor of clover filled the air. The sunshine on the water made Sunny think she was in Heaven.

The annual pot-luck church picnic was a highlight of the year. Folks in the valley looked forward to the first Sunday in September. From afternoon until sunset the folks ate, played games, and sang. The food was placed on long tables in the meadow surrounding the church. Each family brought his own plates, forks, spoons, and drinking glasses. Big Ma made two huge pots of chicken, biscuits, and her famous dumplings. Em made six or more pies. The Jones family was known for making the best lemonade.

The picnic folks watched and sang as the tiny kids joined hands in a circle and played Ring Around the Rosey. Here is the song.

> Ring around the rosey
> A pocket full of posey,
> One, two, three, four,
> We all tumble down.

Hide the Thimble for the small children brought laughter for everyone. The child in the center of the circle was blindfolded while the thimble was passed around the circle. When the blindfold was taken off, the child guessed who had the thimble.

The boys flew kites and played marbles. Because Sunny had remarkable eye-hand coordination, she excelled at playing marbles. Sunny liked the game of jacks, too. She treasured the silver jacks and the red rubber ball that Aunt Bell gave her in a little gold box.

There were races for children, women, and men. The sack race where you had to jump a specific distance while inside a gunny sack caused the most screams and yells. Horseshoes was a favorite game of the men. Horseshoes were tossed at a stake 40 feet away. The man who could first toss 10 ringers was the winner. A ringer is a shoe that comes to rest encircling the stake. It must not touch the stake.

The Tug of War was fun. Contestants were divided into two teams. Each team tried to drag the other team over the center line. The Water Bucket game caused the most excitement. Two opposing teams ran with containers of water a specified distance to see which team could fill their bucket first. At sunset the tables were cleared and put away. Happy families went home.

Most agreed the biggest highlight of the year was Christmas time. On Christmas Eve Sunny's church presented the story of the birth of Jesus. Sunny looked forward to the box of Christmas hard candy that was given to each child at the close of the performance. Sunny hoped someday to play the part of Mary, the Mother of Jesus.

The Christmas service was one of smiles, not laughter. It was solemn, quiet and filled with praise. Members rejoiced that a

child was born whose message was to love each other. The service
began with the singing of "Oh Little Town of Bethlehem, how
still we see thee lie." Christmas was the only time the white folks
attended their church service.

DON'T FORGET THE BEST

Sunny liked the good times. She especially liked it even better
when Grandma would tell her stories. She liked Grandmother's
story about the donkey best of all. A farmer's donkey fell into a
dry well. The donkey cried and cried. The farmer did not know
what to do. The donkey was old, so the donkey wasn't worth the
effort to get him out. Since the well had to be covered up anyway,
the farmer thought it best to cover the donkey with the dirt as
they filled in the well. He asked his neighbors to bring their
shovels and help him fill the hole.

When the dirt first came into the hole, the donkey cried
louder and louder. Then there was quiet. After more shovels of
dirt were thrown on the donkey, the farmer looked into the hole.
The farmer's neighbors continued to shovel dirt on top of the
donkey. Each time the donkey would shake off the dirt, he would
step up higher on the dirt. The donkey continued shaking the
dirt off and stepping up higher until he stepped over the edge of
the well and trotted off. Life is not easy.

Big Ma told Sunny, "As you go through life, you're going to
have a lot of dirt thrown on you. Be like the donkey. Shake the
bad experiences and troubles off your back, and step up higher. It
isn't easy. The donkey didn't cry anymore when he realized that,
even though he was being hit with shovels full of dirt, instead of
letting it cover him, he could shake it off." Sunny knew something
good was happening. Sunny's trust in God would lead her out of
any hole she got into.

At bedtime Big Ma would say to Sunny, "Don't forget the
best." Sunny knew "the best" meant her prayers. When Sunny
left for school, Big Ma said, "Don't forget the best." Sunny knew
that meant God was guiding, guarding, and governing her life as
a prayer for that day.

CHAPTER THREE

ONE ROOM SCHOOL

"The schools of the country are its future in miniature."
Chinese Proverb

"Education, then, beyond all other devices of human origin,
is the great equalizer of the conditions of men
—the balance wheel of the social machinery."
Horace Mann

"Intelligence is seeing things as they are."
George Santayana

Sunny Liked School. Sunny walked to school from God knows where, from over the hills. She never knew how far it was. Her teacher was a man. There were children of all ages. They sat on benches. The one room had a stove, the teacher's desk, and some benches.

There was no trouble in Sunny's school. Sunny said, "If you didn't do what the teacher told you, you got *switched* on the behind with a slender flexible stick or twig from a tree. Another punishment was, you'd hold out your hand, and the teacher swatted your hand ten or more times depending on your disobedience. It wasn't pleasant. Once was enough to make anyone mind the teacher. You would sure think some fire was going on as the teacher hit your hand with a ruler. Another thing the teacher did was make you stand in the corner."

After reciting the Pledge of Allegiance, everyone got busy with their lessons while the teacher started his daily schedule. First the teacher went to the beginning class. The pupils studied numbers and the letters of the alphabet.

The students shared two hornbooks. The hornbook was a piece of wood shaped liked a paddle. On it was pasted a sheet of paper which contained the alphabet, a list of numbers, and the Lord's Prayer. Repeatedly the teacher pointed to the letters and numbers and read them aloud. The pupils repeated them back to the teacher. The teacher had them learn two new spelling words a day. Later he would test them. The pupils studied the letters and numbers while the teacher taught the older students. You were not allowed to whisper or pass notes. He spent more time with the older students. Their lessons were more complicated, and they had more subjects.

When Sunny grew up, she often remembered being assigned the spelling words *father* and *mother*. Sunny did not have a father, so she thought there was no need for her to learn to spell father. She copied the word *father* on her cardboard ruler. The children each had a cardboard ruler made by the teacher. At testing time, Sunny took out the ruler and copied the word *father* on her paper. The teacher flew to the bench where Sunny was sitting, grabbed her paper and ruler, and shouted that Sunny was cheating. He strode to the front of the room and lectured on the evils of cheating.

Sunny was punished only two times. It was by her first teacher. The big boy on the bench behind her pulled her hair and hair ribbon Big Ma fixed on Sunny's head. He waited until the teacher was not looking his way. Then he would give Sunny's hair a big yank. Sunny took the bow off and was trying to fix the bow.

The teacher grabbed the ribbon and gave one of his lectures on not paying attention to your lessons. He tortured her with twelve swats of the ruler on her outstretched hand. He never gave Sunny back her beautiful ribbon. When the class dismissed for the day, Sunny walked by the chalkboard and broke the teacher's perfect, long piece of chalk in half. She skipped down the dusty road home laughing and singing. She was grateful that she had another teacher for the rest of her school days.

The new teacher became a friend to everyone in the valley. When it was time to sell their cotton, he went with the men to the mill to see they were not cheated. He had an outstanding voice and knowledge of music. He led the church choir and organized singing groups in the valley.

In fourth grade Sunny was a member of a girl's quartet the teacher directed. She liked the times when the whole school sang in roundelays. Sunny thought her school was Heaven.

People in the valley came to Sunny's teacher for advice. He helped everyone as best he could. Sunny's teacher loved everyone, and everyone in the valley loved him. Big Ma was not able to buy Sunny books. Sunny would look over the shoulders of other kids. Sunny would give them some of her dinner for looking at their books.

Sunny could beat anyone at spelling. The last thing on Friday, there was a spelling match. Sunny went to the head of her class on *compressibility*. The teacher used the little *Blue Back Speller*. All Sunny had to do was look over someone's shoulder at the words a couple of times, and she would remember how to spell the words.

BOOKER T. WASHINGTON

Sunny's teacher read stories to the class. One story was about Booker T. Washington. He wanted to go to school. Sunny had the desire to learn in school. He was born a slave. He lived on a Virginia plantation in a one-room shack. Booker slept on the dirt floor. Booker T. Washington never knew his birthday.

When Booker was five years old, he was put to work fanning flies off his master's table at mealtime. As he grew older, he was given new jobs like taking a load of corn to the mill to be ground into meal.

Booker longed to go to school, although it was against the law for slave children to go to school. Abraham Lincoln freed the slaves in 1863, but Booker did not know he was free until Northern soldiers came to the plantation and said the slaves were free. The war ended in 1865. Booker was a slave until he was nine years old.

The Booker family moved to West Virginia. Booker worked in a salt furnace. When the furnace boiled the salt out of the water which came up from under the ground, Booker shoveled the salt into barrels. Then he pounded it down. This work was *very hard* work.

Booker taught himself to read. He studied at night. When a school opened for black children, he got to go to school, but not often as he had to work in the salt mine. In his first classroom experience, Booker T. Washington was asked for his surname. He did not have one, so he gave himself a name. It was Washington. At 4:00 a.m. he worked in the salt furnace so he could attend classes at the school. This reward after work is why he thought the classroom was the same as Paradise.

When he was around twelve years, he got a job in a coal mine. He dug coal in underground tunnels which at any moment could cave in. The tunnels were dark and terrifying. He worked many years in the coal mine.

One day he heard two men talking of a school called Hampton Institute where one could go even if they didn't have money. They could work at the school to pay for their education. Booker was sixteen. Although the school was 500 miles away in Virginia, he made it there alone. He traveled by train, stagecoach, and walking. He graduated in 1881.

Booker was chosen to be the principal of a black school, the Tuskegee Institute. The school was in Alabama. Under Booker's leadership, Tuskegee became one of the better schools in America.

Booker T. Washington became a renowned speaker. He said, "I want to see education as common as grass, and as free for all as the sunshine and rain." Booker T. Washington was the first black man to have dinner at the White House. He had dinner with President Theodore Roosevelt.

Sunny's teacher often repeated Booker T. Washington's words.

> More and more we must learn
> to think not in terms of race or
> color or language or religion or
> political boundaries, but in terms
> of humanity.

Booker T. Washington

MOVE FROM THE AVERAGE, TO THE BETTER, TO THE BEST

Sunny's teacher had one copy of *Swinton's Fourth Reader* by Bayard Taylor to teach from. Sunny was impressed by the story of the shepherd and the dwarf because it had Big Ma's same advice; "Don't forget the best."

The story is about a shepherd tending his sheep. While tending his sheep, a poor shepherd picked a beautiful flower. As he picked the flower, he saw an opening in the side of the mountain. He entered and walked down a passageway until he came to a large room. Sitting at a table was a smiling dwarf. The room was filled with gold and diamonds. The shepherd placed the flower on the table. The dwarf said, "Take all you want but don't forget the best." Many times the dwarf said, "Don't forget the best." After filling his pockets, he carried as much of the gold and diamonds as he could. The last thing he heard as he went out the opening was "Don't forget the best."

Out in the sunny meadow, the shepherd noticed the opening in the mountain had closed. The gold and the diamonds were gone. His pockets were empty. He was as poor as before. He realized that if he had taken the best part, the flower, he could have gone into the opening in the mountain again and again. Sunny treasured this story because it had Big Ma's same advise "Don't forget the best."

BENJAMIN BANNEKER

Sunny reminisced, "My teacher would tell us the story of a brilliant black man because it made us feel that we were black and smart, too." Benjamin Banneker was an astronomer, a mathematician, a writer, and an inventor. Most black men and women were slaves during Benjamin's lifetime. Ben and his family were free blacks. Ben's Mother, Mary, was never a slave. His father, Robert, was freed as a young man.

Sunny would softly weep when the teacher told the story of Benjamin's grandmother. Benjamin's grandmother, Molly Welch, was white. When Molly was young, she lived in England and worked for a farmer. A cow kicked over a bucket of milk while she was milking. The milk spilled on the barn floor. The farmer did not believe her explanation and said she stole the milk. He had her arrested. The laws were very strict in England at that time. One of the 300 crimes that could be punished with death was stealing.

Molly escaped hanging because she could read. Around 1683, Molly was sent to a tobacco plantation in Maryland. She was an *indentured servant.* She worked without pay for seven years to pay back the plantation owner who had paid for her boat trip from England. At the end of seven years, she rented a piece of land and grew her own tobacco. In a few years she was able to buy her own small farm and two slaves.

One of the slaves was a charming man who said he was a prince from Africa. He was captured by another African tribe and sold into slavery. Molly did not believe in slavery. She freed the slaves as soon as she could financially. She married the charming slave.

This charming man was Ben's grandfather. The man's daughter, Mary, was Ben's mother. Molly, Ben's grandmother, taught him to read. Her only book was a big Bible she had ordered from England. Ben's school was open for only a few months each year. Students had to help with farm work in the spring and summer. Ben borrowed books and studied in his free time.

When Benjamin was around twenty years old, he was determined to make a clock. He took a watch apart and put it back together again and again. From this practice he got the idea to make a chiming clock. He added a bell that rang on the hour. The clock kept *accurate* time. Most homes in eighteenth century America contained two books. They were the Bible and an almanac. Astronomy became Ben's big interest. He watched the night sky and studied the cycles of the moon for nearly a year. He wrote his findings in an almanac.

Benjamin Banneker was best known for his surveying work. In 1791, Ben helped survey the land for the United State's new capital to be called the District of Columbia. President George Washington hired a man from France to draw the plans. For some reason, the Frenchman quit his job in a rage. Benjamin Banneker redrew the plans from his extraordinary memory. Sunny proudly commented, "Now that's something. This black man gave us the locations for our buildings in Washington, D.C."

Sunny's teacher had each of his students memorize the words of Benjamin Banneker.

> The color of the skin is in no way
> connected with the strength of the
> mind or intellectual powers.
> *Benjamin Banneker*

ONE STEP AT A TIME

Sunny's teacher would often say, "A journey of a thousand miles starts with the first step." Sunny liked the story about the clock in the old *McGuffey's Reader*. The clock had been running for a very long time on the mantelpiece. One day the clock started thinking, "How many times during the year ahead would I have to tick?" The clock counted 31,536,000 seconds in a year. The clock said, "I can't do it," and stopped ticking. Someone reminded the clock that it did not have to tick the 31,536,000 seconds all at one time. It could tick one by one. The clock began to run again and ticked happily on its way one by one. The teacher said, "Take one step at a time, and you will get to where you're going."

A CHRISTMAS CAROL

Sunny learned a lot from the story of Charles Dickens's *A Christmas Carol*. Her school teacher acted out the part of Ebenezer Scrooge. Ebenezer Scrooge was a man who didn't honor Christmas.

Sunny's teacher explained how to advance one's thinking in life. The teacher interpreted what Dickens was saying. The teacher taught, it's the story of our lives. Sometimes we are like selfish Scrooge. At times we are all like Tiny Tim. We can be selfish and lame in some areas of life. Like with Bob Cratchit, we are sometimes victims. Like Mrs. Cratchit, who refused to toast Scrooge, we are too moralistic. We are haunted by the Ghost of Christmas Past sometimes. The Spirit of Christmases to Come teaches us to make better choices that will improve our future life so we become a blessing to our environment.

The moral of the story is that we become generous and sympathetic to the needs of others. If not, our selfishness will destroy us.

Sunny's teacher helped the attentive class to grasp the concept that we live in a world where everyone is connected. The good thoughts we have **improve** the world for everyone. The bad thoughts we have **haunt** the world for everyone.

JOAN OF ARC

For a rural area, Sunny sure was getting some gems for her education. Sunny learned of Joan of Arc from her teacher. Sunny's favorite story of all time was *Joan of Arc*. St. Joan was born in 1412, in the fifteenth century, in the village of Domremy. This teenage, unschooled, country girl freed France from the English occupation army.

Joan was the youngest of five children. Her father, a peasant farmer, was poor but self-sufficient. As a young girl, Joan was known for her obedience to her parents, religious fervor, unselfishness, generosity, and kindness. She would give up her bed to homeless strangers who came to their home asking for shelter. She was a pious child, brave beyond her years. Joan never learned to read or write.

When Joan was about thirteen, she started hearing voices. The call of God was only made clear to her gradually. The voices told her to be good, attend church, and that God would help her. As she approached eighteen years of age, instead of the voices coming once or twice a week, insistent voices visited her daily. The voices told her to go to Orleans. She was to take the Dauphin Charles to Reims for his crowning and to drive the English from the land. Joan made preparations for her campaign. The king offered her a sword. She begged that a search be made for an ancient sword, buried where she directed, behind the altar in the chapel of Ste-Catherine-de-Fierbois. The sword was found in the place Joan's voices indicated.

Joan wore male clothing. She always slept fully dressed. Before she could be employed in military operations, Joan was examined by learned bishops and doctors. A standard showing kneeling angels presenting a feur-de-lis was made for her.

Joan began her mission for God in the company of only six men. Joan of Arc wore armour and unsheathed her sword to rally her troops. After winning a battle, Joan would go out on the field and comfort not only her own men but enemy soldiers as well. In battle she took arrows in the chest, in the thigh, took slashes in both arms. In another fierce battle, she was pulled from her horse and spent a year in captivity. In captivity she was for a time chained by her neck, hands, and feet and was kept in an iron cage. She was allowed no spiritual privileges.

Joan was sold to the English for a sum which would amount to several hundred thousand dollars in modern money. The Burgundians who sold her to the English did not want the English to execute her until they could defame her in the eyes of the French peasants and troops, who regarded her as a saint. She was turned over to the French ecclesiastical courts. Joan was tried on 12 charges of sorcery, wantonness in cutting her hair and wearing men's clothes, and blasphemous pride in regarding herself as responsible directly to God rather than to the Church. After a trial, she was condemned by the church elders as a witch and a heretic partly for hearing voices. She was to be burned alive. She was betrayed by king, by church, by state. Joan was allowed to make her confession and to receive communion. At the stake she asked for a cross. While bound to the stake, her demeanor was such as to move even her bitter enemies to tears. To the last, Joan declared the voices came from God.

After execution her ashes were thrown into the river Seine. In 1920, the Church of Rome declared Joan to be a saint. Her feast day is celebrated on May 30th.

Sunny remembered back to the day her teacher first read Joan of Arc. She told a friend in detail, "It was a stormy day. The thunder, lightning, and sheets of rain terrified most everyone in the schoolroom. It became so dark, my teacher could almost not see to read. So he strode back and forth in the front of the room shouting out the story. I was enthralled.

The storm still raged when school was over. In my imagination, I galloped down the muddy road in my bare feet, charged off on my lean mean war-horse shouting and waving my banner. A blue banner showing a white dove with a scroll on its beak. The inscription read: 'By Command of the King of Heaven.' I would stop on the road and comfort both the wounded English and French soldiers just as St. Joan did.

"By the time I got home, I was captured. I was betrayed by the King of France I had put on the throne, the Bishop, the church, and the civil courts. I was burned at the stake. Until the end, I maintained I'd heard the voice of God directing me."

Then Sunny told her friend, "Like Joan of Arc, I am walking through life now with the glory of God directing, guiding, and shining through me. In the Bible, Jesus says, 'No greater love has any man than this: that he lay down his life for his friends.'

Sunny would say, "The Bible was on the right hand corner of my teacher's desk. He seldom read from the Bible, but my teacher would place his hand on the Bible and recite passages and tell us stories from it. His favorite was Jeremiah 6:16. 'Stand at the crossroads and look; ask for the ancient paths, ask where the good way is, and walk in it, and you will find rest for your souls."

These stories were embedded in Sunny's consciousness.

CHAPTER FOUR

SPIRITUAL EXPERIENCES

"Man can no longer live for himself alone. We must realize that
all life is valuable and that we are united to all life. From this
knowledge comes our spiritual relationship to the universe."
Albert Schweitzer

"The longer I live, the more convinced I am that material
progress is not only valueless without spiritual progress, it is, in
the long term, impossible."
Eugene Holman, president Standard Oil

"God is the ocean, and my prayer is a wave."
Spindrift Research

There Came A moment when everything Big Ma had
been saying to Sunny made sense. Big Ma's faith became
second nature to Sunny, too. Many of Big Ma's qualities were
being repeated in Sunny. She was conscious of the abundance of
her Heavenly Father's gift of love to all the earth.

They say that children are more sensitive to psychic things than adults. Sunny had relatives who came unannounced. Sunny would tell Big Ma and Em in advance that they were coming. There were no telephones. Sunny was able to do this predicting throughout her childhood.

One time when Sunny and Big Ma were going to visit friends twenty miles away, one thing after another kept them from getting started. Sunny said, "Something tells me we should not go." While they were unhitching Old Bill from the buggy, the wheel fell off of the buggy. They both felt that Sunny's perception had saved them from being stranded far from home.

Sunny never felt poor. She was joyous and conscious of abundance. She felt like, "My cup runneth over . . . I shall not want." These words are from the 23rd Psalm. In Malachi 3:10 are these words "Prove me now herewith, saith the Lord of hosts, if I will not open you the windows of heaven, and pour you out a blessing that there shall not be room enough to receive it." Sunny felt that God was like a shepherd watching over her and caring for her.

Folks marveled that Sunny could turn to many passages in the Bible so quickly. It was because she studied her Bible every morning and night before she went to sleep. God was first in her life, and she felt His blessing for her.

Sunny was conscious of the sky, the wind, the fields, the earth, and the grass as tall as a man. She experienced the joy of walking in the muddy paths after a rain in her bare feet and the smell of spring. The sky seemed a part of Sunny. She would often rise early to watch the sun come up and at twilight watch the sunset. Sunny had a mysterious feeling come over her when she saw butterflies.

One spiritual experience from childhood impressed her memory. On a morning when Sunny was skipping down the dusty road in her bare feet to school, she felt a *Stillness* in the air. It was a strange aliveness that engulfed her. This strange *Stillness* permeated her consciousness making her alert to the world around her. She looked around. The grass, wild flowers, and even the stones along the road stood out with brilliant color. Sunny was flooded with a vivid picture that she was not alone. A living consciousness not her own was with her. A sense of good permeated her thought. A bodiless voice said, "Good morning, Merry Sunshine."

She looked around. There was no one there. Some things can't be explained. They are only experienced. As Sunny walked toward school, the vividness of the stones, grass, and flowers didn't remain with Sunny, but a sense of peace remained. For the rest of her life, whenever in trouble, the memory of this spiritual *Stillness* came back to encourage her.

When Sunny was grown, she felt her childhood experience of the *Stillness* related to one of the Bible's depictions of God's presence:

> For ye shall go out with joy, and be led forth with peace; the mountains and hills shall break forth before you into singing, and the trees of the field shall clap their hands. (Isa. 55:12)

Sunny had a peculiar habit. Sometimes she would blurt out the number someone was about to say. For example, a vacuum cleaner salesman came to her door. He came inside and Sunny witnessed his demonstration on the living room rug. He began his pitch. "The price of this vacuum cleaner is just . . . ." Sunny interrupted, "$250." The salesman dropped his jaw; "How did you know I was going to say that?" "Sometimes numbers pop out of my mouth," Sunny said.

When Sunny prayed about the concept of "transportation," she thought of the butterflies and birds; how their tiny wings carried them to where they wanted to go. Sunny was grateful for her location on Wilmette avenue. The public bus went right by her home. One day there seemed to be a practical break about Sunny's transportation needs. A neighbor retired from work. He told Sunny to let him know when she needed to go someplace, as he would be happy to drive her. He wanted something to occupy his time. Sunny felt that now she had wings also and praised God for watching over her.

Several times when Sunny was asleep in her home in Wilmette, an unseen voice would wake her up saying, "Turn on the lights." Each time she would get out of bed, and as she was making her way to the light switch, she would hear someone trying to get in her outside door. When she turned on the light and looked out the window, she would see someone walking away.

One time when Sunny was taking money to deposit in the bank down in the Loop to save for her home, an unseen voice said, "Go to the other side of the street." Sunny went to the other side of the street. Just as she reached the other side, a huge glass window fell from the building right where she would have been walking. Sunny marveled at her safety.

CHAPTER FIVE

TRUE WORTH

"Whatever we beg of God, let us work for it."
Jeremy Taylor

"It is a piece of great good luck when someone
values you at your true worth."
Baetassar Gracian

"There is so much good behavior in the worst of us,
and so much bad in the best of us, that it
behooves all of us not to talk about the rest of us."
Robert Louis Stevenson

Grandma Took Sunny to the Baptist church. Big Ma was a mother deacon. She wore a special blue bonnet which only deacons wore on Sunday. Big Ma told Sunny, "You don't just look your best on Sunday. You look clean, starched, and pressed every day for those you love."

Big Ma gave Sunny a penny every Sunday to put in the collection. Sunny wished it was a nickel. She hoped someday she would be able to put a nickel in the collection. Big Ma saved the *new* pennies for the Sunday collection. Big Ma would say, "Thank you, God, that I have a penny to give Sunny for the collection."

Sunny was sick one Sunday. Big Ma left her at home while the rest of the family went to church.

Sunny decided she would surprise them by having Sunday dinner prepared when they came home. All she could find was a big box of onions. Sunny fixed a bowl of sliced onions in vinegar, salt, and water. She put it on the table. Big Ma saved the bacon grease when she fried bacon. Sunny cut up onions and fried them in the bacon grease. She put a bowl of fried onions on the table. Then she sliced more onions. Sunny put melted butter in a skillet and added flour and milk. She had creamed onions. She put a bowl of creamed onions on the table. She cut up more onions and put them in boiling water with butter and salt and pepper. Sunny put a bowl of boiled onions on the table. She sliced a bowl of plain onions and put them on the table.

When the family came home, they were surprised and laughed. Ever after they told the story of Sunny's five bowls of onions for Sunday dinner.

Sunny converted to God when she was nine. It was during a protractive meeting. Protractive means people went on worshiping for hours. These meetings were the same as revival meetings. The revival part was when the older people would sing and pray. Later they called anyone in the crowd to the Mourner's Bench. They were called up front. When sinners would come there, the Christian people would pray over them. If sinners felt they were forgiven for their sins, they professed their religion. The folks thought Sunny was too young to know the meaning of conversion, but Sunny went up to the altar and prayed. She visualized herself put on the altar. She was not consumed. God preserved her life.

The black folks rarely had a regular preacher at their churches. Most preachers were called *Horseback Preachers* or *Traveling*

Preachers. A Horse Back preacher came through several times a year. The preachers rode from church to church and practiced their sermons on the way. The Tennessee Walking Horses were preferred by the Horseback Preachers because they were fast and steady. When a Horseback Preacher came to the valley, the people rejoiced. They knew they were going to have a feast of love and goodwill.

The Horseback Preachers heard God call them to travel around. The preachers learned the Bible stories. They told the Bible stories as living, life-changing accounts. They could elaborate and improvise on a single story for over an hour. By the end of the sermon, the people were standing, dancing, clapping, and shouting.

On one of such occasion Sunny was baptized. She was baptized in the spring, when the Blueberry River overflowed the banks. Pretty but haunting blue water moccasins were in the river. The preacher's strong arms held Sunny's back as he plunged her backwards into the river. Sunny never forgot those blue water moccasins floating around as she was baptized.

Most Sundays at twilight the neighbors would gather to sing. They would look up at the big house and serenade the white folks. The white folks were on the hill on the west side of the plantation. They would yell, "What are you going to sing for us?"

"What do you want us to sing?"

"Those old hymns you sing in church."

The valley was filled with happy voices singing "When The Roll Is Called Up Yonder," "The Old Rugged Cross," "Abide With Me," "Rock of Ages," "The Battle Hymn of the Republic" and other spirituals. The black folks clapped hands, some laughed, some cried, rejoicing together. The white folks enjoyed the singing and sent down a treat.

Sunny was a high soprano. The white folks said Sunny sang like Patty Brown and should study in Europe. She didn't know anything about Patty Brown or Europe. Sunny knew they were complimentary, but she didn't know what they meant.

CHAPTER SIX

CLOUDS

"Living is struggle . . . no life is so hard that you
can't make it easier by the way you take it."
Thornton Wilder

"No one can make you feel inferior without your consent."
Eleanor Roosevelt

"Believe that life is worth living and your
belief will help create the fact."
William James

There Were Some folks who were not real aunts and uncles.
They were close folks called aunts and uncles. Aunt
Charlotte had consumption. Em went to take care of Aunt
Charlotte. Em did not get paid. She cooked, washed, and sewed
for no pay. Folks just helped each other out. Aunt Charlotte's
husband, Mr. Potts, was coal black, tall, hard of muscle with the

vigor and strength of field folks who had spent their lives in the outdoors plowing, chopping cotton, and hoeing potatoes. Mr. Potts had six children. The children were light colored. All six had sandy brown hair. Aunt Charlotte was half white. At night when Mr. Potts came in from the fields, he would throw Em up on his horse and say, "Take my horse to water, gal."

Aunt Charlotte talked to Sunny's mother Em and told her, "Doctor said I won't live long. I've got only one piece of lung. Em, I want you to marry Mr. Potts and take care of these children because you are such a good seamstress."

Em said, "Aunt Charlotte, I don't want that old man. He's old enough to be my daddy. These children are in their teens."

Aunt Charlotte said, "Yes, Mr. Potts is old, but I want you to finish raising these children for me and sew for them.

When Aunt Charlotte passed on, Em didn't want that old man. Em went back to live with Big Ma and her daughter, Sunny.

Mr. Potts managed to persuade Em to live with him and care for his children. Em cared for his children and left Sunny with Big Ma.

Em didn't marry Mr. Potts. When she started having children from Mr. Potts, she was overworked. She came to Big Ma's and stole Sunny to help take care of the children. Sunny was thirteen years old then. The morning Em came to steal Sunny, Big Ma had stepped out somewhere. Em took Sunny in the horse and buggy to the home of Mr. Potts. When Big Ma came home and found Sunny was gone, the next day she went to her school and took Sunny back home with her.

Em and Big Ma had a wrangle over where Sunny was going to live. Em won. She took her daughter to live with her to help out at the Potts' home. When Sunny went to live at the Potts home, she didn't get to go to school anymore.

Sunny longed to be back with Big Ma. Most of all she missed going to school. Her teacher tried in every way to convince her mother to let Sunny continue in school. Grandma knew how sad Sunny was, but there was nothing she could do.

The teacher didn't give up, and Sunny didn't give up either. The teacher had only a few books in the classroom. He found a way to send Sunny books. The story of Booker T. Washington comforted Sunny. She resolved to follow in his footsteps. Even if she wasn't in a school, she was going to study and read whenever she had time.

Mr. Potts didn't treat Sunny fairly. Sunny could see the difference. The first wife's children were always better than Sunny. When Mr. Potts bought supplies at the commissary, he'd buy good stuff for his own children and shaggy stuff for Sunny. He worked Sunny like he worked his boys. His girls were ladies, but Sunny was a plow girl. Em would fuss about Sunny but to no avail.

Sunny tried to follow "Trust in the Lord with all thine heart; and lean not unto thine own understanding" (Prov. 3:5) She repeated "When thou passest through the waters, I will be with you." (Isaiah 43:2)

Sunny felt she was passing through the waters. She didn't know when, but she kept on praying that God would deliver her. When she worked in the fields, butterflies kept her company and gave her peace.

At dusk Sunny came in from working in the fields. She went straight to the outside pump, took the metal wash pan, and scrubbed herself. On Saturday night everyone in the family took a bath in the large, tin tub so they would be clean for church the next day. On Monday that same tub with a scrub board was used for washing the clothes. On an outside line Em hung the sheets and clothing. The air made them have a fresh smell.

In the back of their home was an outhouse. This outhouse was used in the daytime. At night inside there was a container used and emptied every morning. That is why later in life, Sunny thanked God in her prayers for providing the advanced ideas of inside toilets, toilet paper (Sunny's family used Sears & Roebuck catalogues), washing machines, and for inventions that made life easier.

While working in the fields, one of Potts' boys would come along with a whip and make Sunny's horse go faster. When Sunny got to the end of a row, Sunny would say to herself, "Never mind, Sunny. When I get grown, I'm going to leave."

One of Mr. Potts' boys was Jim. Jim thought he could win in a fight with Sunny. Jim hit Sunny. Sunny beat Jim up. Sunny told Mr. Potts, "Yes, I beat him, and if he bothers me again, I'll do it again. I'll not only hit him, I'll hit you."

Sunny knew her mother made a mistake. That is a reason, when Sunny was grown, she would tell young girls in church they would be crazy women to marry a man with a family and raise his children for him. Two sets of kids don't get along.

One night Sunny heard her Ma, Em, say, "Stop that, Potts. Stop that!"

Sunny was a light sleeper. She raised up and heard Potts abusing her mother. Sunny didn't have anything on but a dress and drawers. Folks didn't have underwear like they have now. Em and Potts went out the front door. Sunny got up and went out the back door. Potts had Em down in the horse lot, his hands around her neck choking her. There were some cedar roots around a big wash pot that was used for boiling water to wash clothes. Sunny grabbed some cedar roots. She went behind Potts. She wasn't tall enough to hit him on the head, so she jumped up and hit Potts on the side of the head. It scared Potts so, he jumped over the fence and ran.

Em didn't know Sunny was out there. When Em did find out what happened, she yelled to her brother Bird. Potts' house was in a valley surrounded by hills. When Em yelled "heoo," the voice would echo. Brother Bird heard Em and yelled back "heoo." Bird got on his mule and came over. Em told him what happened. Potts told Uncle Bird that Sunny was trying to kill him. Sunny said that was true because he was choking her mama, and she didn't want Potts to kill her mama. Bird told Mr. Potts that he'd better not touch Em again or he would kill him.

When it came to work, Sunny outworked the Potts' children. They were jealous of her, especially Jim. Workers make rows to set out potatoes. Sunny could set out the potatoes very fast. In April when setting out potatoes in the field, Jim came behind Sunny and pulled out every other potato. Sunny would have to go back and set the potatoes out again.

One day Sunny warned, "Now you pull up another one, and I'm going to pull you up and put you down!"

Jim waited awhile, then came up behind Sunny and pulled up another seed potato. Sunny got a stick and went after him. She couldn't catch him, but she could throw like a man. The stick got tangled in his feet and threw him down. There was a fight.

When Mr. Potts showed up, he got a shrub and hit Sunny across her mouth. When Sunny came home, Mama said, "What's the matter with your mouth?" Sunny could not tell her because her mouth was so swollen.

Em questioned, "Potts, what you do to my Sunny?"

He replied, "She and Jim was fighting. I aimed to hit Jim, but I hit her."

Sunny yelled, "He didn't! He hit me!"

Em screamed to Potts, "Well, you and me are gonna have it!" They did.

Sunny's mama bellowed, "I'm going to take Sunny over to Big Ma, and Sunny's not going to help here no more. Potts, I done raise your children for you, and now I'm raising another set for you, and you're trying to kill my child."

Sunny was a pretty good size when Em took her back to live with Big Ma. Sunny stayed with Big Ma where she was better off.

Potts' boy, Jim, ran off. Potts didn't know where Jim was. Sunny didn't know either, and she didn't care. Living at home was a joy. Sunny liked living with Big Ma and Big Ma's mother, too. Sunny's great grandmother.

CHAPTER SEVEN

TROUBLED TIMES

"Perhaps even these things will some day be
pleasant to remember."
Virgil, The Anenid (19 BC)

"People with great troubles talk about little ones,
and the man who complains of the crumpled rose leaf
very often has his flesh full of thorns."
G. K. Chesterton

"Life consists not in holding good cards but in
playing those you do have well."
Josh Billings

Sometimes Sunny's Ego got in the way. She stood up for herself when she should have listened to her elders. When Sunny believed she was old enough to get married, she married one of her schoolmates, Silas Westhill. Her mama and Big Ma told her not to marry this boy. The boy's family pushed Sunny to marry Silas Westhill. Em said his mother wanted another plow hand and knew Sunny was a strong worker.

Mama wouldn't go to the wedding. Em didn't know if Sunny was married or not. Sunny was married in the preacher's parsonage at twelve o'clock.

Sunny's elders were right. Sunny's husband Silas didn't treat her right. Silas' daddy had yoked the cow and her calf. This was to keep them from jumping over the fence and going into the neighbor's plantation. When Sunny was seven months pregnant, she was milking one of the Westhill's cows. Sunny had to sit on a box when milking the cow. As she was milking the cow the calf bumped the cow—WHAM. The cow kicked Sunny over and stepped on her stomach. The cow couldn't get her foot out of Sunny's new dress. The cow's foot was still on Sunny's stomach when Silas' brother, Albert, who was milking four cows down from Sunny, came over to dump his milk in Sunny's pail.

He said, "What's the matter?"

Sunny couldn't say anything because the cow had knocked the breath out of her. Albert set Sunny on the box. Then he carried her up to the house. She was delirious and in pain. Sunny's mother-in-law gave her a cup full of caster oil and turpentine. That was when Sunny lost her baby.

The loss was hard. Sunny had to learn to give her baby up. Sunny had a dream of a graveyard. Her sister, Fredona, was digging piles of dirt. Talking to Fredona, her great grandmother, who had passed on, kept exclaiming, "What a beautiful baby." Sunny woke up. The only times she could stop crying was when she thought of her baby being in heaven and happy with her great grandmother.

Sunny was constantly in pain. She had a pan under her day and night as the blood kept flowing. Silas' mother and sisters took care of Sunny. Sunny's condition didn't improve. She became weaker each day.

One day Sunny's husband, Silas, asked if she wanted to go for a ride to the commissary. She did. Lil was Silas' sister. Lil put towels and cloths under Sunny. Silas carried Sunny to the buggy.

Sunny thought they were going to the commissary to get groceries. Silas had to go through the woods to go to the commissary, but the horse and buggy were going the other way. Sunny became alarmed. When she questioned her husband, he said, "You are sick. My mother and my sisters don't want to wait on you any more. You are going to your Mama's. It would be good for you to be with your own folks."

Sunny cried, "What will Mama say when you bring me home like this? She didn't want me to marry you and didn't come to the wedding."

Silas growled, "I'll bring you some groceries tonight."

"You aren't going to bring me groceries. You are telling me that because your daddy said I was a sick hen and wasn't of any service to you because your cow kicked me and stepped on my stomach. I don't want you to take me up to Mamas." Silas wouldn't listen.

When they got close to Mama's house, you could see the house in the distance. That was close enough for Silas. Silas shouted *whoa* to the horses. He said to Sunny, "I can't take you up to your mama's. She won't like it, and we will have a fight."

Sunny was sick and was carrying her stomach in her hands. Silas put Sunny off on the plantation by the big road. Her husband set her on the grass and left her. Sunny's sisters saw her. Her sisters came to her. Sunny was left on a small hill, and Mama's house was on a big hill. The sisters locked hands. Sunny sat on their hands and put her arms around their necks. They took her up to her mama's house. Sunny's mama, Em, screamed and yelled. Boy, did Sunny ever get it! She gave Sunny the devil about Silas.

Em shouted, "You come back here with your belly in your hands. Silas' family won't do anything for you now! I told you they were no good. They wanted you for a plow hand. They used you up. Now they don't want you. They threw you down. Now they are giving you back. I tried to get you not to marry a Westhill."

Sunny said, "Oh, Mama, I wish you wouldn't tell me all that."

Em scolded, "You were the only dog in Westhill's kitchen. I'll tell you that as long as I live."

That hurt Sunny. Sunny never could forget that word *dog*. It was so bad for her mother to call her that. Sunny did come to realize that she didn't listen to her elders. If she had, she wouldn't be in a mess.

Silas had a child by another woman before he married Sunny. Sunny's mother knew it, but she couldn't get Sunny to listen. Silas didn't marry the woman, but he got a divorce from Sunny and married another gal. He had eight children by her.

Sunny didn't want to stay with her mother. Old Mr. Potts was still living then. Sunny was carried to the buggy and driven up to Big Ma's. Big Ma lived about twenty miles away from Potts' farm. Big Ma welcomed Sunny with open arms. Day after day she prayed and cried over Sunny. She asked God to guide them and bring a healing. Sunny was the most limpish thing you ever saw. You could see every artery in her body. She was a living skeleton. Sunny looked like she was at death's door. One day she looked in a mirror and fainted.

Early each morning Granrdma and Grandaughter prayed together. Sunny felt each day the unfoldment of God's plan. The Bible told her to think not of tomorrow, but just to take care of God's will today. "Take therefore no thought for the morrow; for the morrow shall take thought for the things of itself." (Matthew 6:34).

Big Ma turned to Isaiah 40:31: "They that wait upon the Lord shall renew their strength; they shall mount up with wings as eagles; they shall run, and not be weary; and they shall walk, and not faint."

Sunny's favorite verse was "Fear thou not; for I am with thee: be not dismayed; for I am thy God: I will strengthen thee; yea, I will help thee; yea, I will uphold thee with the right hand of my righteousness." (Isaiah 41:10).

Good news came gradually. Sunny would soon stand upright and walk slowly without help. Big Ma's sister, Lucinda, came down from Memphis to visit. She had not seen Sunny for years.

Lucinda also told Sunny that God would heal her. Lucinda quoted the Bible, "Is any sick among you? Let him call for the elders of the church; and let them pray over him, anointing him with oil in the name of the Lord, and the prayer of faith shall save the sick, and the Lord shall raise him up." (James 5:14, 15.)

Sunny said, "If God would heal me, I'd serve Him for all my days."

Sunny's Aunt Lucinda had a verse she had Sunny memorize.

> Wherever you are, be noble,
> Whatever you do, do well,
> Whenever you speak, speak kindly,
> Give joy wherever you dwell.

CHAPTER EIGHT

GLORIOUS MEMPHIS

"Prayer is a corridor for unseen solutions."
Spindrift Research

"To be loved is the best way of being useful."
French Proverb

"I know well that happiness is in little things,—if anywhere; —but it is essentially within one, and being within seems to fasten on little things."
John Ruskin

In 1910, Sunny was twenty-three years old. She was weak and sick. She had a continual flow of blood for three years. Auntie Lucinda wanted Sunny to live with her in Memphis. Sunny moved to Memphis. Auntie Lucinda kept telling Sunny God would heal her. Sunny told her auntie over and over that, if God would heal her, she would not turn her back on Him for the whole round world.

Her auntie took Sunny to the service at the Saints' church. The church was directly across the street from where Aunt Lucinda lived. When Brother Mason called for the sick people to come up to the altar, Sunny went up. The Saints prayed for Sunny. The next Sunday Sunny didn't go to the service because the flow of blood was so great. After the service, Brother Mason and Brother Smith went to Lucinda's home and asked why Sunny wasn't in church. Lucinda told them her condition.

Brother Mason said, "In the Bible when the woman had the twelve year issue of blood, did she stay home or was she among the people trying to touch the hem of Christ's garments?"

That did it. When Sunny heard Brother Mason speaking of the woman with the issue of blood, she cried out, "I have the issue of blood!" She told the brothers that her schoolteacher recited a poem by the poet John Greenleaf Whittier.

> The healing gift God gives to them
> Who use it in His name;
> The power that filled the garment's hem
> Is evermore the same.

Sunny accepted that Brothers Mason and Smith had the healing gift from God. Sunny knelt down. Brothers Mason and Smith prayed over Sunny. One brother laid his hands in the middle of her back and the other on the back of her neck. They rebuked the demons of death and infamy. They asked Jesus to make Sunny whole. They told Sunny to go in peace and sin no more.

Sunny believed when they said to go in peace, she should have gotten up. Sunny didn't get up. The brothers kept on praying and saying Amen. Amen means—*This is the Truth.*

Sunny didn't say a word, so Brother Mason told Sunny to open her mouth and praise the Lord. Brother Mason insisted, "Say *thank you* to Jesus. You can't get anything in a jug with a stopper in it."

Sunny began to say, "Thank you, Lord."

When Sunny came back to earth and knew anything, the Brothers were gone. She told Auntie that Brother Mason said she was healed.

Auntie said, "Well, God does a finished work."

Sunny told Auntie, "If I'm healed, I'm going in and clean up."

That was on the 28th of September. Sunny never saw any blood until the 4th of March, when the issue of blood returned. Sunny was thinking about it though. It was a beautiful, clear, cold day with the sun shining. Sunny thought she felt something, so she went in and looked. Her Auntie affirmed, "God does a finished work . . . God doesn't do parts . . . He finished it whole." In March Sunny was permanently healed. It was like cleaning a house. You clean all of it. After her healing, Sunny often prayed, "You are such a wonderful God. You healed me and saved me. I mean to serve you as long as I live because you brought me from a long ways off." Sunny went to the Saints' church and prayed there from that time on.

WORKING IN MEMPHIS

After her healing, Sunny got a job. She rejoiced that she could do day work. She also wanted to learn. Everything was different in Memphis. She'd always lived in the country. When you scrubbed floors, you just threw buckets of water on the floor and used a broom. In Memphis, you get down on your knees and scrub.

At one house, a lady asked Sunny to open the door to the furnace. Sunny went downstairs and looked and looked. When she came back, she said, "I don't see no furnace. What is a furnace?" The lady took Sunny downstairs and showed her.

Then the lady took Sunny upstairs and showed Sunny the chain you pull upstairs to open the door to the furnace. Sunny did know how to make a fire in the fireplace. For some of the ladies, before she went home at night, she'd lay the fire in all the fireplaces over the house, so the rooms would be warm all night.

Sunny was fired one or two times because she would not tell a lie about different things. One was over the water bill. If you didn't pay, they would cut your water off. In one of the homes where Sunny was working, they had curtains on the front door. You could pull them apart and see who was there. The bell rang. The lady told Sunny to go to the door to see if it was the water man. Sunny was to tell him that she was not home. Sunny said, "I can't tell him you're not home."

Sunny went to the door and said, "Mrs. Hoover said to tell you she ain't home."

He said, "Tell the lady I'm going to cut the water off if she don't pay the bill."

Mrs. Hoover told Sunny, "You go home. You didn't say what I told you to."

The best job Sunny had in Memphis was as cook for the employees of the Breeze and Block Dry Good Store. Sunny made $7.50 a week. That was the first time Sunny ever made that much money in her life.

THE ARRIVAL

Sunny's sister, Mattie, came up from Mississippi. Mattie had a man with her. Sunny didn't know Mattie ever had a man because Em never allowed any of the children to stay out after sundown. Sunny remembered you had to come inside when the sun was at the top of the trees. You'd better *be* at home, or your behind was beaten when you did come home.

Mattie wasn't married. Mattie's stomach was large. She was going to have a baby. Mattie didn't get married. Sunny took care of the new baby.

Sunny believed she was saved. She didn't have to run out with men. When men promised Sunny great things to get her to go out with them, Sunny didn't believe them. Sunny stayed with her Auntie Lucenda. Sunny was glad she did. If God hadn't saved her, no doubt Sunny would have done the same thing as her sister. Sunny had the spirit of God no matter how much men offered her. She told herself, "No thank you! Sunny doesn't need it. I am saved."

BUCK BUCHANAN

In Memphis Sunny met Buck Buchanan. Buck was a smooth talker, dandy dresser, and handsome. He wore a big diamond on his left hand, a diamond stick pin, and a diamond watch. He flashed a roll of bills at people as if he had all the money in the world.

The Saints saw Sunny and Buck going out together. They told Sunny, "He's not saved. You're going to get into trouble again. You have no business with that unsaved man. If you hook up with this man, you are not going to heaven. It's gonna be h-e-l-l. If you pray, the spirit of the Lord will show you these things." Sunny paid no attention to the Saints.

Sunny did not know until after she was married that Buck had a two year old child by one of the women he was running with. Sunny should have heeded the advice of the Saints.

Sunny's Saints' church was called the Sanctified Church. Buck's was the Methodist Church. Buck was a class leader in his church. In the Methodist Church they have class leaders who go around to see if any members are sick or troubled. It seems that different church denominations disagree about who is saved.

Sunny found out that she wanted a husband like other women. Sunny was hardheaded about this marriage like she was with Silas Westhill, her first husband. World War I was on. Buck was from Alabama. He was in Memphis dodging the army. Buck thought if he went to Chicago, they'd send him out to war from there. He didn't want to go to any of the Southern camps.

Buck did go to Chicago. It turned out that Buck Buchanan didn't have to go to a boot camp. He got a job in Chicago and sent for Sunny. Buck and Sunny got married on the 28th of November, 1916.

CHAPTER NINE

CHICAGO

"All happy families resemble one another,
each unhappy family is unhappy in its own way."
Leo Tolstoy, *Anna Karenina*

"Do not depend upon others: there is no grace,
no help to be found in the outside."
Buddha

"The happiest life is that which constantly exercises and
educates that which is best in us."
Hamerton

B uck Was True to Sunny when they first got married for
over a year. Buck was a presser in a tailor shop. They
rented a room for $3.50 a week. They used the ladies' kitchen
for their meals. Sunny would make Buck's breakfast, roll his
lunch, and then he went to work. Life was fine.

Buck didn't want Sunny to work outside the home. There were so many things Buck and Sunny needed. For a long time, Buck didn't know Sunny was working. Sunny would slip outside and work for half a day. She worked for three teachers who taught in the Chicago schools. The teachers lived in three separate apartments in the same building on the same floor. The building was east of Cottage Grove on Ellis in Hyde Park. Sunny cleaned their flats and made nine dollars a week. Each teacher paid Sunny three dollars. That's how she bought her linens and silverware.

Sunny attended the Saints Church on the south side of Chicago. She cherished her memory of the inexpressibly glorious day in June when she was baptized for the second time. Before the baptism Sunny attended an all day revival meeting. At twilight about twelve members sang hymns as they walked to the shores of Lake Michigan. The Saints wore white robes. The preacher stood waist high in the lake water. The eloquent preacher plunged the white robed Saints under the water. Sunny took her turn. She felt filled with perfect love, joy, and peace after being submerged.

Sunny reflected on a particular sermon. Brother Daniels gave a sermon about a black man in ancient Africa. This large, powerful, bad tempered man from Ethiopia was a murderer and thief. When he and his gang of seventy-five robbers attempted to rob a monastery, he was overwhelmed by the kind, warm, peaceful manner of the abbot. He sincerely repented of his past sins and begged to remain at the monastery.

One day an angel appeared to this man with a tablet full of his sins. As he confessed each sin, the angel wiped the tablet clean until the tablet was completely clean. This black man left his evil ways behind him and became a monk. He was a Christian chosen for priesthood and was ordained.

This priest was known as St. Moses the Black. Berber nomads killed him during a raid on his monastery. St. Moses refused to defend the monastery. He decided he would rather die than go against the admonishment of Jesus to turn the other cheek and defend himself.

Sunny said, "I learned in church that St. Moses misinterpreted what Jesus meant by turning the other cheek. Brother Daniel preached that to not protect yourself was against how Jesus acted. Jesus Christ overturned the tables of the moneychangers and drove them out of the temple. Jesus was not a passive man. Jesus fought evil." Brother Daniel read a Bible translation he liked better. "Don't react violently against the one who is evil." Brother Danel said, "Jesus is not telling us not to resist evil. The lesson was, don't turn into the type of person you hate."

Brother Daniels' sermons were mostly about being loving, but there were times to be tough, too. He preached forgiveness. The way to have a peaceful life is to forgive all those who have hurt you in some way. It was a hard assignment for Sunny to forgive people in her past. Forgiving Buck was really hard. Sunny found it difficult to live that way. Sunny tried to live each day knowing that God was guiding her and helping her to forgive the past and to forgive Buck for running around with other women. Sunny would admit that when it came to forgiving, she was no saint.

Sunny often remembered Brother Daniel's remark, "We need to separate in our knowledge, who is a saint and who is an ain't."

LIFE CHANGES

When Sunny felt homesick for her grandmother, Big Ma, and Mississippi, she would make Big Ma's fried apples and biscuits. She fried a few slices of bacon, then poured off some of the grease, and added sliced cooking apples with the skin on. Then she added a little water, brown sugar and cooked them until tender. This food helped Sunny feel less homesick.

Easter was Sunny's favorite holiday. Buck would take Sunny to see the decorations at Marshall Fields. Sunny and Buck had lunch in the Walnut Room. The hot peach cobbler with ice cream was their delight. The last time they were there, waiting for the check, Sunny felt the Stillness. This presence was with her and slowed the room down. She turned to Buck, "Big Ma is dead."

Her head sank. Big Ma was more dear to her than her own mother or Buck. She thought if only she could have been with her.

Buck thought Sunny had food poisoning for saying such a thing about Big Ma. Sunny turned to the same God her grandmother loved. Sunny reached out to this Stillness, this divine source of comfort and love. No words. Just reaching out to her Savior. Spiritual ideas came to help comfort her anguish. She recalled, "I will not leave you comfortless; I will come to you." (John 14:18)

As they walked through the store, they passed the china section. Sunny's tear-filled eyes glanced at a butterfly mug. She bought the butterfly mug on impulse. Holding the butterfly mug close, she felt comforted.

Sunny felt God's continuing care of Big Ma. A loving warmth encircled her. Buck did not say a word. He thought she was going out of her head. Sunny made her way home with some peace in her heart.

When they got home, the phone rang telling them of Big Ma's passing. Buck said, "Sunny, you are a most peculiar person. You were miles away, but you knew when your grandma passed on. You're spooky."

Sunny remembered that someone told her that butterflies were a sign of ascension. Butterflies made one realize how precious and delicate life is and how one should savor each moment and enjoy the little things. Butterflies symbolize transformation.

In the weeks that followed, Sunny clung to each assurance of everlasting life from the Bible. It seemed as though a change in her consciousness was happening. A small ache lingered. She longed for the missed opportunity to tell her grandmother how very much she loved her.

Sunny began attending the Christian Science Church on Sundays and Wednesdays. *Science and Health with Key to the Scriptures* is the book they read from on Sundays along with the Bible at the Christian Science Church. She recalled something she'd read on page 1 of *Science and Health*. "Desire is prayer; and no loss can occur from trusting God with our desires, that they may be moulded and exalted before they take form in words and in deeds."

When Sunny dreamed one night, she found herself telling her grandmother that she loved her. She heard the words "I KNOW." Her consciousness was flooded with warmth, an enveloping love and that Stillness again. When she awakened, she felt that God was communicating to her and to her grandmother. They both sensed how much they loved each other. She felt in her innermost being the words of the Apostle Paul. "For I am persuaded, that neither death, nor life, nor angels, nor principalities, nor powers, nor things present, nor things to come, nor height, nor depth, nor any other creature, shall be able to separate us from the love of God, which is in Christ Jesus our Lord," (Rom. 8:38, 39)

Whenever Sunny's grandmother came to her mind, it was with joy and assurance that her grandmother was cared for by God. Both Sunny and her grandmother had the same Love of God around them. Sunny could feel the meaning of the words in *Unity of Good 37:11-13*. "Because God is ever present, no boundary of time can separate us from Him and the heaven of His presence . . . ."

Sunny told Buck, "I never knew a better person than my grandmother, Big Ma. She was clean in thought and in language. I never knew her to utter a slang expression only once. She was working with a window that was stuck in her home. She used a stick to hold the window up, and thought she had it so the window stayed up. It was a window that pushed up and down. It came down full force on her fingers. I heard her say 'darn.' I was so surprised that grandmother would say such a word, my mind was only full of my grandmother saying 'darn,' and not that her fingers were hurt. I've remembered that experience."

Sunny mused about how our thinking regarding language has changed. Big Ma told Sunny that using foul language was a form of killing all those people within earshot. Sunny thought it was true. The language on TV today is helping to destroy the good behavior we have in our world and in such a subtle way people are not aware of what is happening to them.

Sunny remembered her grandmother telling her that in 1842 when Big Ma was 15 years old, she made a covenant with God that once a day she would try to read to understand some portion of the Bible. She would keep the example of Jesus before her mind and endeavor to act according to her knowledge of what Jesus would do. Sunny tried to follow her grandmothers example.

* * *

As part of her wages, Sunny and Buck got their own flat above the restaurant where Sunny worked. The flat was large, so they took in roomers. Sunny worked downstairs with the owner of the restaurant. His wife was the cashier. Sunny was the cook. The Buchanans lived in the flat two years and four months. Then trouble began. Buck went home to bury his brother. His sister, Pearl, asked him if her daughter could come to Chicago and live with Sunny and Buck. Pearl wanted her daughter to attend the Wendell Phillips High School near them.

Buck wrote Sunny a letter, "Pearl wants Lizette to come back with me so she can go to school at Wendell Phillips High School. What do you think?"

Sunny wrote Buck back, "Yes, let her come."

Immediately on arrival Lizette was trouble. Lizette was an unruly girl. Sunny couldn't do anything with her. When Lizette came home from school, she was supposed to come downstairs and help with the vegetables and dishes. She rarely came downstairs. One day Sunny heard her walking upstairs and waited for her to come down. When she didn't, Sunny went up to get her. The back door was locked with the chain on. She went to the front door. It was locked with the chain on. When she went bam, bam, bam on the door and pushed the door far enough with the chain on, she saw Lizette come out of Robert's room. Robert was their roomer.

Sunny hollered to her, "Come open this door!"

Lizette opened the door. She didn't look right. Sunny said, "What you doing in Robert's room?"

Lizette said nothing. Sunny said, "I'm telling your mother you ain't doing right."

Buck came home from work. Sunny told him what had happened. Buck said, "Well, I'm going to send her back to her mother. Pearl wouldn't want her getting herself spoiled up here. Pearl would not like that one bit."

Lizette wanted to fight. Sunny told Lizette, "You're not going to fight me in my own house. You're going to get out of here."

Buck said, "No, I'm going to take her out. I'm going to put Lizette on the train."

He took her and put her on the train. When Lizette got home, she told her Mama a pack of lies against Sunny. From then on her mother wrote to Buck but never to Sunny.

CHAPTER TEN

TURBULENCE

"It all depends on how we look at things,
and not on how they are in themselves."
Carl G. Jung

"Everyone is a prisoner of his own experiences.
No one can eliminate prejudices—just recognize them."
Edward R. Morrow

"Life is a dream, and it is well that it is so,
or who could survive some of its experiences."
Isadora Duncan

Buck's Sisters, Pearl and Ruby, came to Chicago. They arrived in Chicago in August 1919, the same day the Chicago race riots began. The riots started with stone throwing on two Lake Michigan beaches between 26th Street and 29th Street. At the 29th Street beach, there were vocal and physical demonstrations against a group of blacks who wanted to use the "white" beach. A single white man threw rocks at two colored boys on a raft. One of the boys, Eugene Williams, drowned. Rioting escalated when a white policeman refused to arrest the white man who threw the rocks. Instead the police arrested a black man. These episodes led to five days of rioting which took the lives of 23 blacks and 15 whites, and 291 people were wounded.

Sunny hooked the lock and the chain on their door. Buck was working outside Chicago in Argo in a salt factory. Buck tried to come home, but the riots were going on. He could not get home the first night. The next night when he came home, Sunny had the lock, and the chain on the door. Sunny asked how he got home. Buck said he came home by 39th Street. When Pearl, Ruby, Buck and Sunny were worrying about the riot, Buck turned to Sunny and said, "If anyone bothers you, you tell Pearl."

Sunny replied, "Why should I tell Pearl? I ain't married to her. I won't tell Pearl nothing. I'll tell the man who wears the blue coat and brass buttons." Buck put his confidence in his two sisters, not in Sunny.

The Alabama folks were all so close. They had a club where they got together, played cards, drank, and talked about all the expenses Buck had to handle by himself. The two sisters were in Chicago only a few days when Buck came to Sunny and said, "My sisters have been talking to me about all the expenses I have. You'd better get you a full-time job instead of helping out in the restaurant."

Sunny told him, "I thought you didn't want me to work full-time?"

He said, "Pearl and Ruby can take care of the house since there're here."

Sunny said, "I'll get nothing! They'll get out of here. That's what they'll do."

Sunny thought she'd better get a job. She put an ad in the paper. She got a job with a woman who had a candy store called the Vendome on 31st and State Street.

One day, when Sunny came home from work, all the Alabama folks were having a fling-ding. The tables were full of beer bottles and glasses. The room was so full of smoke Sunny could hardly see. Sunny thrashed through the smoke to the kitchen. She was furious. This was her house. She was home and tired after working all day. She put down her groceries and walked through the smoke to her bedroom. She changed to a loose fitting dress, took off her shoes and stockings, and wondered how Buck could be so different when his sisters were around. Try as she could, she could not quench the anger that swelled up inside her. Sunny's room and the room Buck's sisters had were next to the living room. Sunny heard the Alabama folks leave. She stayed in her room. She wondered how much beer Pearl and Ruby drank.

When Buck came home, he didn't come to Sunny's room. He went down the hall to his sisters' room. Sunny followed him and said, "Why are you going down there? You don't belong down there."

Buck said, "Pearl and the Alabama folks told me you said for me to get out."

Sunny said, "I meant get Pearl and Ruby out of here. When they go, joy go in front of them and peace behind them."

Sunny went back to her room. She was cutting her toenails with a razor when the sisters came cussing at her. They might have been drunk. Pearl shouted a lot of bad words. Pearl came with Sunny's chair and hit Sunny over the head in Sunny's own house. Sunny grabbed that chair and whacked the devil out of Pearl. Sunny cut her with the razor. Pearl had fifteen razor strokes around her body.

The police came and took Sunny down to the 35th Street station. Sunny never went to jail. The Lord delivered Sunny. Buck went against Sunny. He left Sunny for Pearl and Ruby. When the day came for the trial at the police station down on Harrison Street, the white woman with the candy store where Sunny worked came to Sunny's aid. She was a wonderful woman.

The candy store woman said, "No two women can be boss of one house. That was your husband and your house. They had no business being in there." She got Sunny a lawyer and stood with Sunny.

The judge asked the policeman, "Who arrested this woman?"

"I did, your honor."

"What kind of a home did she come out of?"

The policeman answered, "My home doesn't look clean like hers. She had plaques of the Lord's supper and other religious plaques all around her house. I've been on the force for thirteen years. I've never seen a cleaner house."

The judge said to the matron, "Take this woman upstairs and examine her head. See if she has any soft spots."

The lawyer told the judge, "The candy store owner who hired me told me that before these people came from Alabama, her husband didn't want her to work. But after they came, he asked her to get a job. She got a job, and they took over the house. Then they had a big fight."

The judge witnessed Buck throw the keys at Sunny. Sunny told the judge she had roomers, and there were all kinds of stuff at her house that belonged to them.

She added, "There is nobody to care for the roomer's stuff but me. My husband and I were buying furniture from Hartmans and Spiegels on time. He's walking away. He's leaving me and ain't going to be living with me. I have to see that these people get their stuff as best I can."

The judge said to the policeman, "I want you to take this woman down to her house and see after her stuff."

The policeman answered, "Your honor, I have to get my dinner. It's 2:30 now."

"What time can you take her down there?," the judge asked.

"My leave is for a hour-an-a-half for dinner. It will be about four o'clock."

The judge said, "You meet her at her apartment at four o'clock, and if anybody bothers her, bring them back to me dead or alive!"

As Sunny left the courthouse, she said to the candy store woman, "The judges eyes were as crossed as two sticks. People used to say cross-eyed people were bad luck, but he was good. This judge was no bad luck."

The woman smiled at Sunny. The policeman arrived at four o'clock to see that Sunny got safely into her house. Sunny could see the lights were on. She knew she did not leave the lights on. Sunny had the keys, but she was too nervous and had to ring the bell. Buck Buchanan opened the door and was surprised to see Sunny. He said, "What does this mean?"

The policeman said, "That's what I'd like to know! I've been on the Chicago police force for thirteen years, and I've never known anybody get this kind of leave after they were sinners—then to come home." The policeman added, "Mrs. Buchanan has other people's stuff she has to see after. You said you did not want her."

Buck Buchanan, two sisters, and two of his friends were in Sunny's flat. They were in there eating the food Sunny had cooked. When they saw the policeman, they beat it out of there. That left Sunny in the house by herself. She stayed in the house alone that night and prayed. She prayed to God to deliver her from going to jail.

When she dozed off for a few minutes, the Spirit woke Sunny up saying, "It's all right, it's all right." The Father had made it all right. Jesus had accepted Sunny, making salvation sure.

Some of the Saints told Sunny that if she told the judge what she had done, the judge couldn't let her go free. Jesus told Sunny it was all right. When Sunny went back to court, the judge told her that she was free. She wasn't going to jail.

Sunny didn't have an apartment or room any more. She stayed wherever she worked. Buck lived with his sisters for two years. One day Buck showed up and begged to come back. Sunny knew Buck ran around with other women. He claimed he would not run around anymore. Sunny knew better, "You can't teach an old dog new tricks." Because her wedding vows said "Till death do you part," she took Buck back. She had some troubled times with him, but she took care of him until he died.

CHAPTER ELEVEN

PLOWING DAILY LIFE

"Ignorance is a cure for nothing."
W. E. B. Du Bois

"A journey of a thousand miles starts with the first step."
Anonymous

"The most powerful single force in the world today is neither
communism, nor capitalism, neither the
H-bomb nor the guided missile
—it is man's eternal desire to be free and independent."
John F. Kennedy

The Year Was 1921. Sunny worked for an Armenian doctor at 2900 Indiana Avenue. Buck and Sunny lived in a huge house with the doctor. Sunny made the doctor's breakfast, sterilized the instruments and kept the medical room clean. Sunny acted like his medical assistant. She handed him the medicines and instruments he needed.

A man came in with a cut on his finger. The doctor asked Sunny to hand him the witch hazel. He put a dash of that on the cut. Then he had Sunny hand him the alcohol. He doused the cut with alcohol. He had Sunny hand him the gauze and bandage. Then he asked the man for $3.50. Sunny asked the doctor, "You used a dash of witch hazel and a bit of alcohol. How come you charge $3.50 for that?"

The doctor said, "Damn fool, he ought to know how to do it himself. You pay for being a damn fool."

Pregnant women would be silent and walk in the back room. The doctor told Sunny to stay out of the room. She knew what was going on. Sunny could hear them scream. When they came stumbling out of the back room, Sunny had hot tea for them. They usually cried as they drank the tea. Sunny told the women that God loved them and would take care of them.

Occasionally the doctor would have Sunny work at night. A society woman would come in and go in the back room. Sunny remembered that when the daughter of a local politician came in, the doctor was paid extra money. The doctor was so happy about the hundreds of dollars he was paid that he gave Sunny fifty dollars that night.

The doctor told Sunny she would no longer have a job with him if she told anyone what he was doing. Taking the life of an unborn child was illegal. The doctor would be given a jail term for such an operation. Sunny never opened her mouth to anybody. In the 1920s, most people didn't even know the word *abortion*.

The doctor needed a pill maker. So Sunny made the pills, just like she made a cake. All the pills were the same recipe. She put all the different ingredients in. They were nothing but epson salt, soda, and junk. Then she put them in different pans, just like putting eggs in an egg carton.

The pills were little bitty things. Some were round, and some were long. The powder got hard. Sunny used a tiny paint brush to paint the tops of the pills. She painted some green, some brown, and some pink. They looked like tiny Easter eggs. The doctor was a schemer.

When she asked the doctor about the pills being nothing, he said, "That's what some people get for being ignorant."

Sunny's mama, Em, wrote her. Em complained about the man she worked with on the Mississippi land halfers-hands. The man took everything she owned. When she wrote Sunny that he'd taken the mules she was paying for, Sunny decided to borrow the money from the good doctor and bring Mama to Chicago.

Mama left Sunny's brother in Mississippi because he was old enough to fend for himself. Ma brought Sunny's two young half sisters. Fredona was thirteen. Bertie was seventeen. Sunny earned $65 a month working for the doctor. She rented a three room flat for $27 a month for them. This flat was a block away from the doctor's house.

Sunny went to a furniture store on State Street. She spent her savings on over a hundred dollars worth of furniture. She bought a davenport made of brown leather which opened out. Now her two sisters had a place to sleep. This davenport came with two brown leather chairs. One was a rocking chair, and one was a sitting chair. Sunny bought her Mama a bed with a brass frame, dresser, and rug. For the kitchen she purchased an Acorn gas stove with a glass window on the oven door, so her mama could see the bread rise when it baked. Sunny bought a Gibson Ice Box so her mama, Em, could get ice right off the wagon. She bought an enamel table with a drawer for the knives and forks. Sunny was intelligent with money.

Sunny sent the money for the train tickets to Chicago to her trustworthy school teacher. He bought the tickets and made sure that Em and the girls got on the train with the instructions she'd sent. Sunny bought warm coats and sweaters with instructions to wear them.

Sunny got her behind whipped bringing them up here. She waited for them at the station for over two hours. She went back to the house and told the doctor they hadn't come yet. He said three people were in the basement with the janitor. A taxi driver saw them get off the train. When Mama showed him the paper with Sunny's address, instead of waiting for Sunny, for $1.50 the driver drove them to the doctor's home. The doctor had them wait in the basement. The women were shivering from the cold. Their warm clothing was locked in the trunks which they didn't get until three days later. Sunny had to buy them more warm clothing until then.

The women arrived on a Sunday. On Monday, Sunny took out a Metropolitan Life Insurance Policy for protection on each one. She also took them to the beauty shop and had their hair straightened out. The three women were from the countryside, from the sticks. They didn't know a street from a road. When Sunny sent them to the grocery store for salt, they went to the drug store. When she sent them to the drug store to get Lennox soap, they didn't know what to ask for. They could not remember. They always made soap at home. They didn't know what sweet soap was. Sunny bought her sisters books and sent them first to Forest School on 39th Street and later to Wendell Phillips High School.

In the 1920's there were plenty of $2 bills. Sunny would send a note to her Mama written on a piece of an old paper bag and enclose a $2 bill. Mama would see the note and put the paper bag down. Sunny would find the $2 bill still in the bag.

Sunny would say, "Lord have mercy, Mama, you don't pay attention."

Mama said, "I wish I'd stayed in Mississippi."

Sunny hoped that one of her sisters would come to the doctor's house to help with the scrubbing and sweeping. Neither sister wanted to come. The younger, Fredona, finally said she'd come. Sunny took a bucket and mop and told her, "Come on up. I know what to show you." Sunny showed Fredona how to get on your knees and scrub with the brush, then take the mop, wipe it up, and wring it out in the bucket. Then Sunny went downstairs.

Minutes later, the lady that lived below Sunny came running. She screamed to Sunny, "You left the water running in the bathtub. It's all over my house."

Sunny rushed upstairs. Fredona had her dress tied up around her waist. She was wading in water and swishing the mop back and forth.

Sunny yelled, "Fredona, you done pour the water on the floor! Why didn't you do it like I told you?"

Fredona stared at Sunny, "I ain't gonna get down on my knees. I didn't come to Chicago to work."

Sunny exclaimed, "How'd I afford to get you up here if I didn't work? You don't want to know nothing. I can't teach you nothing. Go home!"

Sunny knew there is no way to teach anybody unless they want to learn. Fredona just didn't want to learn. It's the same with school. Money doesn't make the difference in a school. You have to have personal discipline and students who want to learn. Sunny never went any further than fourth grade, but she wanted to learn. She read and studied every day.

Once after working all day, Sunny brought Mama some money. When they were in the kitchen, Sunny said, "Mercy me! What is the matter with the top of the ice box? It looks like someone took a knife to it."

Mama replied, "The girls have been cutting bread on it. They needed a place to cut the bread."

Sunny exclaimed, "Mama, I bought you an enamel table to cut the bread on."

"Sunny, you is too particular for me. I wish I stayed in Mississippi."

"Mama, I don't wish that you stayed in Mississippi. If you wish to go back, I wouldn't give you a red copper to send you back, but I can tell you how to get back." Sunny gave her directions. "Mama, I'm at 2900 Indiana. Go north to 12th Street. The Illinois Central train station is on your right. You go in there and ask, 'Could I go down on the I. C. tracks and walk south until I get to Mississippi?'" With that, Mama kept quiet.

Another time Mama asked to do bundle washing. Sunny said, "All right, a friend of a lady I know needs someone to do washing. I'll take you there. You can bring the clothes home and wash them in the basement. I'll go with you."

They went to the 43rd block and picked up the bundle. Then Sunny said, "I'm going on to work. Here is the street car going North on Indiana. You take it back home. Get off at 31st and Indiana."

"I know. I get off where the candy stick is turning," Em said.

When the street car came to 31st and Indiana, Mama was busy looking at the houses and missed her stop. She went on to where the car turned west on to 39th to 43rd to the stock yards. The end of the line.

Mama said to the conductor, "Where am I?"

"You're at 43rd and the stock yards, lady. End of the line."

"I want to get to 31st Street."

"Get on this other car. It will take you back to 31st."

Mama was so busy looking at the houses, she didn't watch the numbers. She didn't see where the candy cane was either. She went to Ellis Avenue to the end of the line. The conductor said. "Ellis Avenue. The lake. Far as we go."

Mama said, "My God, where am I now?"

"Where do you want to go?" asked the conductor.

"To 31st where the barber shop is with the candy cane outside."

"All right, I'll put you off there."

Em got off at 31st with the conductor's help. She was clutching her bundle of wash. But instead of walking north on Indiana, she started back to the lake. When she was many blocks from home, Sister Nelson saw her and said, "Where you going?" Sister Nelson walked Mama back home.

When Sunny heard about it, she said, "No taking you to any more bundle washing. I'll take the washing back. I do know a woman who wants someone to iron. I'll take you there. She pays $1 a day."

In the morning Sunny walked Mama to the apartment building. Sunny showed her mama the number to push, and then she went on to the doctor's to work. Mama ironed all day. When Sunny came to take her home that night, Mama was waiting out in front of the flat and told Sunny she was paid only fifty cents. When Sunny turned to go into the flat to ask the lady, Mama said, "No, this is the flat I was in." She had ironed all day for the wrong lady.

Sunny said, "Mama, you don't listen. Your mouth goes all the time. You have one mouth and two ears which means you should listen twice as much and do less talking. You always say I'm high minded, but, Mama, I listen."

Mama blurted, "What do you mean I don't listen?"

Sunny said, "Mama, listening is thinking. Thinking is when your mouth keeps shut, and your head keeps talking to itself.

Sunny tried to help her mama, Fredona, and Bertie, but dealing with them was a hardship.

CHAPTER TWELVE

ACCUSATIONS

"Love all, trust few."
Shakespeare

"Misfortunes one can endure—they come from outside,
they are accidents. But to suffer from one's own faults
—oh! there is the sting of life."
Oscar Wilde

"If a man take no thought about what is distant,
he will find sorrow near at hand."
Confucius

The WPA, the Works Progress Administration, refers to many agencies established by the Federal Government in the mid 1930's. President Franklin D. Roosevelt's administration established the WPA. It began in 1935 as an independent agency funded by Congress. The WPA was the government's project to provide employment for the jobless. It was created to bring the Depression under control. The WPA employed approximately one-third of the nation's 10,000,000 unemployed, paying them $30 to $50 a month.

During the time the WPA was on and when people were on relief, Sunny and Buck Buchanan rented an apartment on 29th Street at 6429 St. Lawrence. Sunny and Buck had two bedrooms, so they took in a roomer. They really didn't want to take this woman because she had a little girl. Ruth was a "quick widow." A woman whose man quits her and leaves her with a child to raise is called a "quick widow." Because Ruth and her husband were separated, they didn't know what the consequences would be renting her a room. Ruth worked at the stock yards. After school, her little girl stayed across the street with a friend until Sunny came home.

Buck was working as a janitor in the Chicago Loop close to the First National Bank. Sunny had been down the street buying clothes off a bargain counter.

Sunny told her roomer, Ruth, about the bargains. Ruth went to a friend of Sunny's and told her that Sunny had showed her a lot of clothes and must have a lot of money.

Sunny continued going to the Saints church. She was also reading Unity. Then one Sunday, Sunny went to the Christian Science Church on 44th and Michigan. It was the Sunday when Ruth and her husband came to rob the house. Buck was sick that Sunday and didn't go to church. They must have sensed someone was there because they didn't rob the house. When Sunny came in the door from church, she heard the ice box open and heard Ruth say, "They must have a lot of money cause she bought a lot of new clothes." Ruth's husband, who was separated from her, was standing there with the little girl in Sunny's house.

The next day when Sunny came home from work, she walked downstairs to the landlord. "There's no heat. What are we going to do?" He didn't answer. Sunny went back upstairs, and soon she could smell smoke and heat coming up.

That evening the doorbell rang. Sunny asked Ruth to answer the door. Sunny had her hands in dough. She was making biscuits.

Earlier Sunny heard Ruth answer the phone and say, "No, they're not here."

She wondered who Ruth was talking about because Buck wasn't home, but she was. Ruth answered the doorbell. Sunny heard someone walking up the stairs. Sunny rolled the dough off her hands. She went to the door and said, "What is it, please?"

"There's been some mistake about the heat, and we're looking for the owner."

Sunny said, "I'm the wife. My husband hasn't come home yet."

When Buck came home, Sunny said, "Men are looking for you about the heat."

The landlord lived downstairs. Buck went to him. When he didn't come back, Sunny said to Ruth, "Where did Buck go? If the devil was a doctor, he'd die before he got back."

Sunny made the biscuits and had pork chops ready. Buck didn't come back. The phone rang. Sunny answered. The man asked, "Is this Mrs. Buchanan?"

Sunny replied, "Yes, it is."

He said, "I was at the police station on 63rd and Dorchester. Buck was arrested."

"Arrested for what?" Sunny yelped.

Ruth was in the bedroom with her little girl. Sunny shouted, "Ruth, did you hear that? Mr. Buchanan is arrested!"

Ruth mumbled, "I don't know anything."

Then Ruth took her little girl and went outside. Sunny realized those two men were plain clothes policemen. All the time Sunny thought Buck was talking about the heat, they'd taken him down to the 63rd Street police station. Sunny wondered why he was arrested. On her table were a 1945 *Christian Science Sentinel* and a Unity booklet. She prayed and read from each booklet. Both of the booklets said almost the same thing. "It wasn't so." Whatever reason Buck was at the station, Sunny knew it wasn't so. Sunny knew something wasn't lining up with the truth. Isaiah 65:24 came to her, "And it shall come to pass, that before they call, I will answer."

Sunny went down the street to the home of the Precinct Captain, Mr. Page Rezena. He was colored. Mr. Rezena wasn't home. His wife told Sunny he went to 55th Street to a wake because a friend of his had passed on. Sunny told her that two men came upstairs. When she asked them, "Are you policemen? they said, "No, we're looking for a man about the heat." These two men were plain clothes policemen. Sunny believed Buck was in the basement talking to the men about the heat. Mrs. Rezena said in the morning she'd get Page to go down to the jail.

That night Sunny read the Bible. She also reviewed the *Sentinel* which said, "It's Not So." Sunny kept that *Sentinel*. Whatever Buck was arrested for, Sunny knew it wasn't so. When Page came the next morning, he told Sunny that Ruth had sworn out a warrant saying Buck had raped her child. Sunny told him it wasn't so.

Page asked, "What's she got that you haven't got?"

Sunny replied, "She ain't got nothing, but she ain't saved, and the little girl is just a nine year old child. It isn't true what Ruth said."

Page said, "I don't believe Buck Buchanan would do such a thing."

Next morning Sunny was to be in court at nine. She looked at the clock and saw she was ahead of time. It read 7:30. Then she went out on the street and found out it was after nine. Ruth had turned Sunny's clock back. Sunny called a taxi and got to court. Ruth was sitting with her little girl. Sunny got there just as Ruth and the girl had sworn Buck was guilty.

Sunny walked up to the judge and said, "It's not so judge. I have proof. I got twenty-five dollars here. If Buck done anything like that, I'll pay twenty-five dollars to the matron to examine the child and see."

Sunny paid the twenty-five dollars. The matron examined the little girl. Nothing bad had been done to her. There wasn't a thing wrong. The judge set Buck free. Ruth beat it down the stairs and went home. Sunny told Buck to take a taxi and get there before she did, to lock and chain the door. Sunny didn't want Ruth to get her things out. Buck just got home in time to lock the door, before Ruth tried her key. The chain was on. She couldn't get in. He peeked out the window and saw her walking away.

Sunny said, "Well, it's over with." But it wasn't over. Ruth swore out another warrant and said Sunny had met the child on the street and molested her and had beaten the child. After Ruth grabbed the child and ran out of the court, Sunny never saw the child again. The court didn't even call the case. In addition to the twenty-five dollars Sunny paid for the examination, she paid four hundred and some dollars that she had saved for the lawyer and the bondsman for Buck. People told Sunny later that Ruth had a terrible time with her daughter. Sunny didn't have to wonder why.

CHAPTER THIRTEEN

QUESTIONABLE CHOICES

"As a man chooseth so is he."
Emerson

"The difficulty in life is the choice."
George Moore

"Dost thou love life?—Then do not squander time,
for that is the stuff life is made of."
Franklin

Sunny Wasn't Interested in other men besides Buck. The thirty-six years they were together, Buck ran around with other women. Women would even tell Sunny what Buck bought for them. It didn't shake Sunny because of her faith. She said, "Let him buy. It's a higher price than he thinks."

Sunny confided to her friend, "I tell you I've been through it. Buck had done me so bad. After all his bad treatment, I stuck to my promise 'till death do us part.'"

Her friend asked, "Was Buck honest enough to confess it to you?"

Sunny thought, "No, but he told friends of mine that I was a good wife, a good woman, a clean woman, and I did this, that, and the other for him."

The friend said, "Why couldn't he have told you himself?"

Sunny agreed, "Buck said he didn't deserve my good treatment. He should have said these compliments to me. Instead he talked behind my back. He confessed it that much. I just hope and pray he made it to Heaven. I sure had enough of that man. I don't want a candy man. I don't want a cookie man made like a man. No, no! I'm through with him for life. He's gone now. I don't have to marry no more. I never had anyone on him, and I don't want anyone after him."

Sunny went on, "God delivered me, and He doesn't have to do it again. He made it possible for me to get this home and the wisdom to take care of it. God takes care of me. All the 36 years Buck ran around, I didn't bother. Let him buy hats and bootleg so he could bring whiskey over to their place. Let them have it. I don't want it. I don't go around to their doors and see, though I was tempted to. I stayed with God. I expect to stay with Him all the days of my life. Sunny felt it was her duty in church to tell the young women not to be married to unsaved men.

She testified, "I know from experience. Get a husband that is one of your own kind. If you marry a man who is good looking and telling you the moon is made out of green cheese, don't believe that lie. You'd better pray and ask God about him first. If you don't, you're going to have h-e-l-l. It's not going to be h-e-a-v-e-n either. Don't you girls marry an unsaved man, a man who doesn't live the Christ. You better stay out of there. When you go off from your home and live in an apartment by yourself, you are inviting trouble. When you make yourselves liable, you have to stand the consequences. You go marry an unsaved man, and you just unequally yoked yourself to a jackass!"

One girl asked Sunny for advice. Sunny suggested, "Try to get the man that has the same mind that you got, if you want to get along."

Sunny told Buck she would not marry him if he smoked. "My Buck made like he was going to be a sanctified man, clean and set apart. He was even going to give up smoking. One day I was looking out the window, and I thought the man I saw looked like Buck. When he got close and rang the bell, I pushed the button and let him in. He came on up. It was Buck."

I said, "What's the matter, dear?"

He whined, "Oh, I'm so sick I don't know what to do."

I said, "What's wrong?"

Buck complained, "I just come from the doctor's office. He told me I had a heart something or other, and I'd have to give up smoking."

Sunny continued, "He quit smoking cigarettes after the doctor told him it was against his heart. When he told me, I said, 'Thank you, doctor. Thank you, Jesus.' But I was disappointed. Buck hadn't quit! The cigarettes made Buck sick, and the cigars made **me** sick. He hadn't quit, but he dodged around and told that lie. He didn't quit."

I told him, 'That's all right. God will get you."

+++++++++

Buck Buchman was a Pullman porter running to Canada and bootlegging. Buck used his legal job to break the law. He used his Pullman train for bootlegging. Buck would bring his liquor back on the train to the United States and sell it.

Sunny said to him, "Buck, don't bring no liquor in here. I don't believe in it. You didn't believe in it either, but here of late you believe what other people tell you."

Buck sarcastically, "Sunny! Robertson bought a home through bootlegging. My friends ain't all that strict about the law."

Sunny replied, "Well, I'm not Rosie, and you're not Robertson. I don't want no bootlegging done in here. I won't have it."

He hissed, "Why not? I can't have nothing in my house but what you want. You so sanctified."

Sunny consoled, "Darling, you can have God in here. That's what I want. No whiskey, no rented rooms in here where men can bring in their women and women can bring in their men. I ain't going to do that to have a home."

Sunny startled, "I'm not supposed to do that, and you're not either. You say you are a class leader in your church. I'm sanctified and trying to live a clean life. You should thank God I'm trying to live my life for one man."

Buck yelled, "Yeah, you sure so sanctified that you can't do nothing for fun or money. Rosie and them got a home now. They ain't all that strict, and that's why."

Sunny calmly replied, "All right, I pray to God, and He sends in what we need. You're on the road, and you ain't getting but $65 a month. I help you pay all the bills, don't I? I'm working every day. The days that you're not working, I'm working. I run the sandwich car and make money and bring it here to put it into this home."

There were these little sandwich cars on Chicago's streets. Sunny had a good business working with her sandwich car. She had a car on Wabash Street. When she made sandwiches, she also made pork chops and hot dogs. She got home from her cleaning work about 5 o'clock. She'd fry pork chops, hot dogs, and fish and sell them. Sometimes she'd make thirty-five to forty dollars a night. For working all day doing housework, she was paid four dollars.

Buck was claiming he made sixty-five dollars a month. His runs were between Canada and Los Angeles on the Chief. Running wild they call it. He had to go to the train office to get his runs. In the North, they stopped calling making illegal liquor *moonlighting*. Northerners call it *bootlegging*.

Sunny said, "I ain't bringing whiskey in our home. If you do it, God's going to get with you."

One day after work, the Spirit of the Lord told Sunny, "Look under the ice box."

Sunny said to herself, "Why do I want to look under the ice box?"

The ice box had a drain under it. She raised the flap. There was a case of liquor.

When Buck came home, Sunny questioned him, "Husband, what's that under the ice box?"

He said, "What ice box?"

Sunny laughed, then snapped, "Don't ask me what ice box. You bootlegging and bringing liquor in here! You no good. This is God's house, and I'm God's woman. You're supposed to be His man, but you're bootlegging! I don't want that whiskey in this house. I ain't doing that."

Sunny came home from work one day and noticed the closet in the hall where guests put their coats.

The Spirit nudged Sunny and said, "Look in the closet."

Sunny said to herself, "Look in the closet, for what?" Who is in there?"

Sunny needed new mattresses so she bought two new ones. The paper they came in she folded up and stored. She put the paper in the closet under the rod where the guests hung their coats. Sunny went in the kitchen.

Her mind kept after her, "Look in the closet."

Sunny opened the closet door and didn't find anybody in the closet. She looked behind the paper and found a case of liquor.

She thought, "This man of mine is still bringing liquor in here."

When Buck came in from the street, she said, "Buck, you can't bring liquor into my house. My house ain't going to be raided and me be put in jail. No sir! You want my name in the paper selling liquor! Get that stuff out of here, or I'm going to call the police!"

Buck said, "You're too sanctified a woman."

Buck took the liquor a block away to the street where they played pinochle and other games. He left the liquor with a woman he was cheating with. When Sunny walked by, Buck pointed Sunny out to the woman. Buck had told her all about Sunny.

On a day in April Sunny walked to the elevated train station. The sunlight, as it beat upon the sidewalk and buildings, was bright and getting hot. Cars shot past. People going to the train were in front and behind Sunny. Sunny felt peaceful and happy because she was going to get paid for doing what she liked to do. She liked to have the houses she cleaned sparkle with freshness and order. Sunny looked forward to the restful ride on the train from the South Side past Evanston, Wilmette, and Winnetka to Glencoe where she was going to work that day. After Sunny was seated on the train, she realized Buck's woman friend was one seat ahead of her on the train. Sunny could see her reflection in the window. The woman was talking to her friend about her boyfriend and his "old lady" who wouldn't allow him to do anything.

Sunny thought, "Buck bootlegs and brings the liquor to her house. They sell it and have a good time."

When the woman told her friend that he brought her a green tam, and he brought his wife a pink one, Sunny knew she was talking about her. Sunny shivered. Buck's girlfriend had a knife in her hand.

When she got off at Sheridan Road, Sunny said sadly to herself, "I'm glad you got me God. She got the knife. She got the man. They got the liquor, but you got me."

The next Sunday, Sunny went to Buck's church. A buddy of his winked his eye at him and said, "Hi, Buck Buchanan. They tell me your girlfriend had an accident!"

Buck tried to pull Sunny away when his buddy said, "I didn't know you were married."

Sunny didn't say a word, but wondered about the girlfriend. Two days later, Sunny heard about the death of Buck's girlfriend and wondered what happened.

She declared, "She had that knife. The devil got her and the graveyard, too. She got killed. Oh! but God got me, and I'm going to stay with Him."

CHAPTER FOURTEEN

AMAZEMENT

"A merry heart doeth good like medicine."
Proverbs 17:22

"Men are not prisoners of fate,
but only prisoners of there own minds."
Franklin D. Roosevelt

"No one wants advice—only corroboration."
John Steinbeck

Sunny Was Sure that God told her, if she did the right thing, He would deliver her from unhappiness. If she walked upright and spoke the truth, nothing would come against her for too long. Gradually her life would turn around.

A girl from her Sanctified Church visited Sunny. The girl was pregnant and felt the weight of the world.

Sunny affirmed to her, "If you don't believe in Him, you are just out of luck."

Later when Sunny attended the Sanctified Church on State Street, her old school teacher's sister, Mary, said, "Come over and see my brother's wife. She's a preacher, too."

The preacher had a storefront church and called herself a spiritualist.

Sunny said, "You know, we don't believe in women preachers."

Mary replied, "Well, she's a preacher, and she can tell you things."

Sunny told Mary she didn't feel like going tonight.

Mary pleaded, "Come on, I just want you to go tonight."

Reluctantly Sunny went with her. She didn't anymore than get inside the storefront church when Mary brought that woman over to meet Sunny. The woman told Sunny something else.

She said, "Your mama ain't home. No, your mama ain't home."

Sunny questioned, "What is that about? I didn't come here to hear a fortune teller."

The woman replied, "No, you didn't. You came to hear the truth. Your mama ain't home."

Sunny lived a block apart from her mama, Em. On Monday when Sunny was through with work, she went by there. Mama wasn't home. Fredona was there.

Sunny said, "Sister, where's Mama?"

"What you want to know for?" Asked Fredona.

Sunny answered, "Because somebody told me she ain't here."

Fredona grumbled, "She ain't. She's up in Waukegan where Bertie's friend Pansy is."

Sunny was taken off her feet, "That woman preacher told the truth!"

They lived a block apart, and Sunny's mama traveled to another woman's house without telling her, but the woman preacher told Sunny it was so.

Sunny had been pestering Mama for letting her sister, Bertie, date a man who was married.

Sunny told her mama, "Pansy has taken Bertie astray. I didn't bring you up here to have Bertie go with a man who's married."

Mama didn't answer Sunny. It bothered Sunny that her mother, Em, never went to church. She never saw that Fredona and Bertie attended either. They laughed and made fun of Sunny for all her God preaching.

Sunny said, "I got my good traits from my Grandma, Big Ma."

Sunny told her family to no avail, "'Thou shalt not commit adultery.' Bertie is dancing with the devil. She is asking for trouble."

Mama got angry with Sunny, "You not Bertie's mama! I'm Bertie's mama!"

"I know I'm not Bertie's mama. I'm not your mama. I'm your daughter, but I'm trying to help you. You shouldn't let Bertie go out with a married man. Now suppose that man's wife met Bertie sometime. It would be a disgrace."

Mama was so mad at Sunny that she went to Waukegan without telling her. The first time they met, the preacher woman told Sunny that her mama wasn't home. Sunny started praying. That night she had a dream and saw Bertie sitting on the bed with a gown on like a hospital gown. It didn't meet in back.

She wondered, "What is that for?"

She knew Bertie was in trouble.

When Mama came home, Sunny said, "You say Bertie is up in Great Lakes working. What is she doing way up there? What's wrong?" Are Pansy and her husband the cause of it?

Mama Em said, "You're nosey! Don't mess in my business."

Sunny added, "I had a dream about Bertie going with this man. I didn't bring Bertie up here to be a whore and hoe hop with another woman's husband. When is Bertie going to be home?"

"I don't know," Mama replied.

"You all is lying. I'm not calling Mama a liar, but you all is lying, Pansy, Bertie, and that guy Bertie is riding around with after school. There is something wrong here."

Sunny made it her goal to find out. She hung around to catch Bertie when she came home. Bertie arrived all right. She was big as a tic. She'd been out with that married man and was with child.

Sunny blurted, "Bertie, that's the reason Mama said she was your mama, and I wasn't. Someone is going to be a mama. You're pregnant."

Bertie frowned, "I'm grown, ain't I?"

Sunny advised, "Yes, you grown but ain't got no business being with another woman's husband. If you wanted to marry a man, you should get one that isn't tied up with somebody else. If the wife meets you out in the street and kills you, I'd be the one that would have to bury you—see!"

Bertie went ahead and had the baby. Before she gave birth, Sunny saw the baby in her sleep. He had on a cap. Sunny tried to straighten the cap on his head. Each time she'd try to put the cap on straight, he'd turn it around.

To Bertie in the dream, Sunny said, "Most boys don't want you to put their cap on. They'll put it on themselves. If you put it on, they'll move it. That's a boy for you."

Sunny woke up and said, "Oh, God, you've given me a job to do. I have to help Bertie through her problem. I got my folks here, and I've done all I could for them, and they've gone against me. My Auntie Lucinda helped me when I had a problem. I will try."

When the time came for Bertie to have her baby, Sunny went to her mother.

"Where's Bertie?"

"She's in the hospital?"

"What hospital?"

Mama Em replied, "County."

Sunny asked, "It's a boy, right?

"Mama nodded, "Yes."

"Who took her to the hospital?" Sunny inquired.

"Pansy took Bertie there," Mama replied.

Sunny was agitated, "Pansy didn't have the baby. Bertie with that married man had the baby. When is Bertie coming home?"

"I don't know," Mama said.

Sunny started walking toward the front door and said, "I'm going for her."

Sunny got on a street car and went to Cook County hospital. When she got off the streetcar, she could see Bertie. Bertie was standing in a window with a little bitty baby. Bertie was crying. The baby was wrapped up the way they wrap them up in hospitals.

Sunny walked up to her, "What's the matter, darling? What cutie you got? Let me see the little one. Oh, what you got to put on him?"

Bertie didn't answer.

"You're going home, darling. We're going back to Mama now. You're friend, Pansy, took you way off with this man. Where's the man? This is what I get for it. I tried my best to be a good Samaritan for you. You have no clothes for the baby yet? Where's the man?"

Bertie kept crying and didn't say a word. Sunny hailed a taxi and took her sister to Mama's. Sunny bought a blanket and one of those little outfits. Then Sunny went to 63rd Street and bought a layette and put it in Bertie's arms. That was the second sister Sunny had to do that for.

Sunny thought, "God done saved me. If God hadn't have saved me, I would of gotten pregnant like my two sisters. I received the spirit of God, and I mean to keep it. I only had a rendezvous with one man, my husband. I don't need another. No matter how much money a man offers me, how often they come around, no thank you. The temptation is there, but God done saved me."

A month later, Sunny sat in her living room with her sisters and Mama. Sunny wanted to discuss two points with them.

One point was how the new baby out of wedlock was going to affect the family. She discussed how they were going to deal with it. They would manage all right, but it was the second baby born without the benefit of marriage.

The second point Sunny told them was that they needed to learn to be patient. People who don't have patience, don't think of the future. The choices people make, that don't consider what will happen in the future, will sink your ship for sure. Sunny told her family a story about patience. It was a story her school teacher in Mississippi had told.

PATIENCE

Two holy men were walking down a dusty path. The two holy men met an angel. They asked the angel how long it would be before they would be enlightened?

The angel told the first holy man, in a few more lifetimes, he would attain enlightenment. That the man had to live a few more lifetimes made the first holy man unhappy. The man protested that he had been faithful and should be closer to enlightenment than many lifetimes!

The angel told the second holy man that he would attain enlightenment, but it would take him many more lifetimes than the first holy man. The angel pointed to a huge tamarand tree. The angel told the second holy man that after he had lived as many times as there were leaves on the tree, he would be enlightened.

The second holy man jumped for joy when he heard he would be assured of enlightenment. As he rejoiced, a gust of wind blew all the leaves off the tamarand tree. At that moment the second holy man attained enlightenment.

Sunny said to her family, "The second man had natural patience. Drop one leaf at a time. It takes one step at a time to get enlightenment. My joy is knowing that I am on the right road to understanding God. I'm on the way. I will get there. I don't have to wait until I get to my destination to be happy. I'm happy right now."

Her family nodded that they were listening.

Sunny continued, "I have patience. Patience has helped me get to where I am."

CHAPTER FIFTEEN

WILMETTE

"Everybody can be great. Because everybody can serve."
Martin Luther King, Jr.

"I think we Negro Americans have just as many beautiful people
in mind and body, as well as skin, as any other group and
that we have just as many stinkers as any other group."
Thurgood Marshall

"The truth is that all of us attain the greatest success and
happiness possible in this life whenever we use our
native capacities to their fullest extent."
Dr. Smiley Blanton

During The Winter of 1945 Sunny took the train from Chicago to Wilmette. Wilmette is an upper middle class suburb. Sunny did housework in Wilmette. She cleaned a different house each day of the week. Often she had to wait a long time for her bus to the train.

Sunny was prepared not to freeze. First, she put on her breast protection. Sunny's mama said her busts were as long as a cow's. Sunny's protection came clean down over her belly. Then she put on her drawers which is a covering from the shoulders to the hips. Next her wool bathing suit, then her stockings, her bloomers, her petticoat, her dress, and her coat. She was warm waiting on the corner. The others waiting would be doing the shimmy. Sunny never let pride of her appearance freeze her out.

When March came, Sunny was riding through the village on the bus. It was cold as blue blazes. The sky was robin-egg blue. The trees were ice-frozen. Sunny marveled, "Everything is white or ice." Sunny felt she was in a wonderland world.

She said softly to herself, "Whew! Isn't it beautiful? If a fairyland is as beautiful as this, I'd like to go there. Oh, I wish I could live out here in the suburbs."

The lady sitting beside her said, "There are two houses here for sale now. Two colored families live out here that I know. At one time there were lots of colored folks living in Wilmette. About 1915 Wilmette had a wind storm that destroyed all their homes. They were scared and moved to Evanston. That's why there are so many colored folks in Evanston today."

The woman pointed to an old house behind some bushes as the bus passed. Sunny exclaimed, "Oh Lord, it looks like a gypsy camp. It ain't what I want, but where I want. If the Lord gives it to me, regardless of hard wood floors and tile baths, with my strength and favor with the Wilmette people, I'll make it what it ought to be."

When Sunny was ready to go home at the end of the day, this lady and Sunny got on the same bus. The lady said, "My church deacon is the real estate man for that house. I made a mistake. It was not the one I pointed out but its an old store." The two women looked out the window as they drove by the old store. "It's a gypsy camp, too. The curtains are flying out the windows. No paint since God knows when. The shingles are scattered on the roof," remarked Sunny.

The lady pointed, "Look, the windows are broken. Suppose you call the real estate man when you get to the train station. Maybe you can afford this place."

Only emergency calls could go through as the telephone strike was going on then. Sunny put in her five cents at the railroad station. The operator couldn't put the call through. Sunny went to the real estate man's church on Sunday. The real estate man happened to be colored. She made an appointment to meet him at the store Sunday afternoon at 3 o'clock. The way the store looked, it would be normal to get discouraged. If it weren't for Sunny's faith in God, she would have been discouraged.

The man said, "Mrs. Buchanan, don't you want to put some money on it?"

"Well, I have to pray about it," Sunny said. Sunny knew God gave her all the money she had. Right on the money is printed "In God We Trust."

When Sunny was praying about the store, her husband grumbled, "You don't want that old place. We have better stables in Birmingham than that old store."

Sunny inquired, "Honey, where's your money?" All Sunny got out of Buck was a shrug of his shoulders. Buck laughed sarcastically, "You don't need to worry about money. God will pay for it."

Sunny insisted, "I'm not worrying, Buck. I know God gave me all the money I got. The money says, 'In God We Trust.' Where is your trust, husband?"

When Sunny talked again to the real estate man about the old store, he tried to get her to put some money down.

She told him, "Today I've only got twenty-five dollars on me. I'll put that down, but I want a receipt for it written in ink, so you can't spoil it out." She went home and talked about putting the money down with her husband. In a few days the real estate man called, "I've got more calls since you put your twenty-five dollars down."

Sunny insisted, "Go ahead and sell it if lots of people have been calling, but if it's for me, nobody else can get it."

She had about two weeks to pray about it. Her husband was against it. Sunny complained, "You ain't got no money. I'm tired of living in these kitchenettes getting my water for cooking from people's bathrooms. We're getting older. I want to get out of here."

Buck said, "Where am I going tomorrow?"

Sunny said, "If you don't make any preparations, you'll go to the old folks home."

"Who's going with me?" Buck blurted back.

Sunny replied, "I'm doing to you like you done to me."

Sunny continued, "If you work and put some money in the bank, we'll buy a home. Buck, you want a car? I can't live in no car. I ain't got no place to park a car.".

Sunny shrugged her shoulders, "Can't stand no car in somebody else's front yard if they don't want it. Have your own place. I believe in having something for myself."

Buck said, "We too old to buy a home."

Sunny preached, "Honey, how come we are not too old to pay rent?. I've asked God for a place, and I believe He is going to make it possible."

Sunny's 25th wedding anniversary came. People brought gifts to the party. She got fifty dollars. On Monday Sunny asked Buck, "Do you want to go to downtown Chicago with me?"

"What you going to do? Buy me a new coat with that fifty dollars?" Buck retorted.

"Buck, I'm going to the First National Bank so I have a home for my mama and you and me when we get old."

Sunny liked the First National Bank. When you first walk inside the lobby, there is a placard on the wall quoting Henry Ford. It reads, "*Thinking is the hardest work there is, which is the probable reason so few engage in it.*"

Sunny never was told why Buck was fired from his Pullman porter job. For one thing Buck's bootlegging business was finished years earlier. The United States Congress made liquor legal again. After being fired, Buck became a janitor at a bank across the street from the First National Bank.

Sunny took out a deposit box at the First National Bank and put fifty dollars in the box. She got two keys. She gave Buck one key for him to put money in the box. Sunny saved and saved.

When Sunny had $275, she went to the real estate man.

He said, "You'll have to do better than that."

Sunny said, "Give me 90 days."

She saved her money and borrowed one hundred dollars from a lady she worked for. Sunny had the necessary five hundred dollars for a down payment. Much of the money was in twenty-five cents, fifty cents, and one dollar bills she'd brought to the bank in a paper bag.

The store in Wilmette cost $5,500. After the down payment was paid, the mortgage was fifty dollars a month. In order to buy the place, Sunny had to pay old unpaid bills. She paid the water bill of twenty-seven dollars and two cents, the electric and gas bills. Then the electricity, water, and gas were turned on.

Buck was not a business man. He left Sunny to struggle with finances, and she had a struggle! He never put in a cent. Sunny's husband was a spendthrift, but only for himself.

Sunny acknowledged, "Wonderful thing to trust God and to have faith in yourself. God paid for this house." Without knowing it, Sunny was talking about the "human and divine coincidence," she heard in sermons at the Christian Science Church.

Sunny told friends, "When I first bought this house, the local taxes were forty-nine dollars. Now they are $336.02. I wonder what the two cents is for? God has blessed me to have the money to pay my fair share of taxes."

Sunny philosophized, "The Lord has wonderfully blessed me. It does not impoverish us to give. Neither does it enrich us to withhold. You have to open your hands to receive anything so I give. If you don't have faith in God and yourself, you can't get up. People can let you down.

The Buchanan's new house is on the street because it had a storefront downstairs. People lived in the back of the store and upstairs. The place wasn't fixed up with walls. The whole store was only one room. Sunny had rooms built. She partitioned off part of the front and made a front room. Behind the front room near the street, she made a dining room. She made a bedroom off the dining room. She built a kitchen and bathroom. Mr. Walman did part of the work. Mr. Rogal did most of it. They were both white men.

Before hiring Mr. Walman and Mr. Rogal, she fired a black carpenter. She tried to give her people some work, but this man was not honest. He sold Sunny's lumber to that dog veterinarian over on the highway. It was black-market time during World War II. Sunny lived on Chicago's south side during World War I. Because of shortages during World War II, you couldn't buy any building material.

In 1945 Sunny bought her home in Wilmette. Sunny found carpenters to do the work. She gave them the money to buy the lumber, and supplies for her. It was similar with the plumbing. Sunny got the tank from the south side from a black plumber who had a yard. She bought her sink from a white man in Wilmette. He had a store that sold sinks and washing machines. She bought more items when she had the money.

During the time Sunny was fixing up her home, Buck read until he went to sleep. In 1945 Buck no longer worked. He didn't want to help around the house. Buck was supposed to look after the remodeling. When Sunny started to fix up her home, she hired a colored man from Evanston. She paid him three hundred and seventy-five dollars. Sunny had to work to furnish the money for the materials. Buck would sometimes go to the drugstore to get a newspaper. He would give the workman a key. They had their stuff piled up in the front of the store where the guest room is now. Sunny put a curtain across where she slept. Another curtain separated the place where her husband slept near the dining room. That was all the privacy they had. Sunny never slept with her husband after she took him back after he'd gone off to live with his sisters. Sunny did keep her promise to take care of him "till death do us part."

Sunny told people who asked, "Yes, I paid thousands for this place. I went through my money. I reckon the money was more for the refixing than I paid for the house. I used common sense. I bought a kitchen stove from a lady selling out in Evanston. I brought a cabinet from the south side."

Friends would say Sunny was a good manager. Sunny told them, "My home! Oh! I had an awful time with my home. Thanks to God, I got it in order. It seems it's taking its toll now. I can live here until Jesus come though. I made my will so whatever I have will go to different charities and churches. I give two dollars, five dollars, and sometimes more to the charities. On Sunday I give five dollars or more to my church."

The workman put Sunny's lumber on the upstairs stairway. Later he took Sunny's lumber over to the veterinarian's place and built him something with her lumber and furniture. She told him she would not pay him another penny. He could go. After all he got three hundred seventy-five dollars to do the work and didn't finish it.

Sunny said, "I wanted to give my own colored people a chance, and that's how they treated me. I had a black man from the south side do my plumbing. He charged me five hundred dollars for one day's work, and he didn't finish. He stole my bathtub. I took him to court. I got some of my money back."

He said, "I got a small bathtub that will just fit in here. Your bathtub is too big." He took Sunny's bathtub in his truck and brought a little tub back. When Sunny came home from work, she said to Buck, "What is this? It's a horse trough, isn't it?"

"That's a bathtub, fella said," answered Buck.

The tub was so small you couldn't get half of yourself in it. It didn't have any outlet either.

Sunny fumed, "Well, he can't leave it in here. Don't let him put it in. You're going to put it outdoors. I have to get a real bathtub."

Sunny went to Mr. Jensen on Linden Avenue. He sold her a bathtub and sent a man over to put it in. He couldn't do the job right, so Sunny had Mr. Rogel put the plumbing in. Sunny had an awful time with the people fixing up her house.

The colored man put in the pipes. Sunny went to the bank and paid him five hundred dollars. The reason she took him to court is, he didn't do it right. The Wilmette inspectors said the pipes weren't done right. They gave Sunny a warrant for him to come back and fix it properly.

Later Sunny hired a carpenter from Evanston, a white man. Sunny was working for Mrs. Tally. She told Mrs. Tally about her problem with him.

Sunny said, "He does not come and do the work. When I call down to him in Evanston, the maid tells me he is out of town, but the spirit tells me she's lying. He's home. I'm going there after work. If I don't get home, you tell my husband to look for me in some sewer because he might throw me in one because I went after my money."

Sunny rang the doorbell. He came to the back door.

Sunny cried, "You haven't done nothing, and you got my money. When you going to work?"

The carpenter said, "I'll be out there tomorrow."

"Now don't disappoint me. I've lost carfare and money because you don't do the work," Sunny warned.

Sunny told Mrs. Tally that rogue didn't show, so Sunny went to the Better Business Bureau. The white man at the Bureau asked what color was the carpenter.

Sunny said, "It makes no difference what color. A fox is a red fox or a gray fox, but he's still a fox. This white man is a fox. He lied to me."

Sunny gave the Bureau the information. The carpenter skipped town with her money to California. He stole a lot of antique things that were left in the store. The Better Business Bureau said they'd bring him back for five hundred dollars.

"Let him stay in California. God will punish him," Sunny replied.

Sunny took more money and hired Mr. Rogal. He's a good man. He has done all of Sunny's work ever since.

Sunny told a woman at the Wilmette Church. She told Sunny that a similar incident happened to Mary Baker Eddy. When the Christian Science Church was young, her church members had a bake sale. The sale raised five thousand dollars for the church. The treasurer for the bake sale stole the money and disappeared. The church members wanted to take legal action. Instead of legal action, Mrs. Eddy said that God would punish the treasurer for his crime more than what flesh could do. It was a strange perception of justice, but Sunny realized she had done a similar thing.

Sunny asked a practitioner to help her. A practitioner is a Christian Scientist who devotes his lifework to solving problems through prayer. That's how she found Mr. Rogal. She went to Dr. Roberts, a practitioner. He had been a popular pediatrician on the North Shore. When he developed a problem he could not heal medically, he decided on applying Mary Baker Eddy's suggestion of treating problems with prayer.

Dr. Roberts moved his family to Allegan, Michigan where he and Mrs. Roberts bought a bed and breakfast which she ran. Dr. Roberts spent his days studying the Bible and *Science and Health* by Mary Baker Eddy. He was eventually healed through his and a practitioner's prayers. To his delight he was cured. Dr. Roberts decided to become a practitioner. A local farmer heard of his healing and asked him to give some doses of prayer for his sick cow. The cow was healed. The cow was Dr. Robert's first patient treated by prayer.

Dr. Roberts moved to Wilmette where he did his practitioner work from then on. Dr. Roberts had a clear perception of the spiritual laws and order inherent in God, man, and the environment. He felt he was still applying laws of healing. The laws were just more spiritual than before. He helped people by bringing to conscious awareness the spiritual laws and order in the atmosphere of Mind governed by God.

Dr. Roberts kept his medical license up to date even though he was a Christian Science practitioner listed in the *Christian Science Journal.* A doctor who was a Christian Scientist was a rarity, almost an oxymoron. There was a joke which actually had some real-life examples. The joke was, a doctor was married to a Christian Scientist. What the one couldn't heal, the other could.

When Dr. Roberts first considered investigating Christian Science and Mary Baker Eddy, he thought that people would think he was silly. When he would visit a practitioner to ask questions, he would make his appointments at night, so no one knew where he was going exactly. He worked at his medical practice during the day.

When Sunny came to visit him, he asked, "Who sent you?" She said, "God sent me."

Dr. Roberts comforted Sunny. He gave her a little book about two and one-half inches in size and told her to read it. The book was *The Greatest Thing In The World* by Henry Drummond. This book gives an interpretation of the Bible verses which discussed love found in the thirteenth chapter of First Corinthians.

Henry Drummond was a 19th-century theologian from Scotland. He wrote, "Love is the greatest thing in the world, and it is the *summum bonum*—the supreme good." He condemned anger or ill temper as "one of the most destructive elements in human nature."

Henry Drummond says there are two classes of sins—sins of the *body* and sins of the *disposition*. The prodigal son is a type of the first, the elder brother is a type of the second. The faults of the elder brother are more serious than those of the prodigal. The elder brother wasn't grateful for what he had. He was sulking outside his father's door. He was angry. His father was welcoming his younger son home after he had squandered his inheritance. He had an uncontrolled temper. It's Henry Drummond's opinion that *uncontrolled temper* is the greatest sin because it affects everyone. Temper is made of jealousy, anger, pride, uncharitableness, cruelty, self-righteousness, touchiness, doggedness—it creates a loveless soul.

Sunny learned from reading the Bible. Jesus told the Pharisees they were like the elder brother. "*I say unto you that the publicans and the harlots (prodigal son) go into the kingdom of God before you.*" Henry Drummond pointed out that a bad temper is falsely viewed as a harmless weakness not to be taken into account when estimating a man's character.

Drummond wrote, "One's ill temper is often the vice of the virtuous. Many men of noble character are easily ruffled, quick-tempered, or have a 'touchy disposition.' One of the saddest problems of ethics is the compatibility of ill temper with high moral character. Temper reveals an unloving nature.

Drummond quoted Jesus:

> Whoso shall offend one of these little ones, which believe on me, it were better that a millstone were hanged about his neck, and that he be drowned in the depth of the sea.
>
> For I tell you that your goodness must be a far better thing than the goodness of the scribes and Pharisees before you can set foot in the kingdom of Heaven at all!

You have heard it said to the people in the old days, "Thou shalt not murder," and anyone who does so must stand his trial. But I say to you anyone who is angry with his brother must stand his trial; anyone who contemptuously calls his brother a fool must face the supreme court; and anyone who looks down on his brother as a lost soul is himself heading straight for the fire of destruction.

So that if, while you are offering your gift at the altar, you should remember that your brother has something against you, you must leave your gift there before the altar and go away. Make your peace with your brother first, then come and offer your gift. (Matt 5:20-24 The New Testament In Modern English—J. B. Phillips)

On Doctor Robert's advice Sunny studied Henry Drummond's little book and waited for guidance. Sunny was lead to study the word *angry* as it appears in the Bible. She came to understand that this undesirable and unnatural behavior disturbs those around us. **Worse, anger disturbs the world's peace. World peace is actually individual peace extending out to the world.**

In the 1970's, Sunny thought about Martin Luther King, Jr. Her favorite quote was, "Darkness cannot drive out darkness, only light can do that. Hate cannot drive out hate, only love can do that."

Another quote Sunny liked was by Patricia Monaghan, "The point of wisdom is not simply to do well...it is to do good."

Unlike living in Chicago, Sunny rarely stood very long at the corner near her house for the public bus to pick her up. Wilmette is a wealthy village. Often someone came by in a fancy car, saw Sunny, and drove her to the L railway station or store. She had a scheduled ride to church.

Sunny's neighbors liked talking with her. They would bring her samples of fresh bread, cake or pie. Mr. Larson across the street liked to fish. He would give Sunny so much fish that she had to share it with friends. During the holidays she was always remembered.

Occasionally the folks Sunny cleaned houses for asked, "Sunny, how is it that you can understand what you read in the Bible, and it's a mystery to me?"

Sunny replied, "I'm a saved woman. It's the Christ that I listen to. I pray. I study. Then I listen." One woman asked Sunny what to pray for. Sunny answered, "It's not the human mind but the Christ Mind which gives you understanding. That is why I pray, 'Let this mind be in me that was also in Christ Jesus, to do unto others what I would have them do unto me and to be merciful, just and pure.' That's a Mary Baker Eddy prayer." The woman wasn't pleased the prayer was by Mary Baker Eddy. She called Mary Baker Eddy the Christian Scientists' high priestess.

Sunny said, "Well, you asked me."

The woman replied, "Yes, I did. Maybe I should consider its worth."

Another employer asked, "What does it mean in the book of Corinthians when it says, 'Look not at the things which are seen, but at the things which are not seen?'" (II Cor. 4:18).

Sunny answered, "I guess the Bible is telling us that the world is not what we think it is. You need to look beyond the fog covering life as all matter to the Truth. In Genesis it tells us that God made man and everything good out of Spirit, not what you see as matter. That's the Truth. It's a hard teaching. The things we see are not seen."

The woman said, "I heard that the *Talmud* says, "We don't see things the way they are. We see them the way we are."

Sunny smiled when she heard the *Talmud* quote and said, "Most people don't believe that, but will learn through hard knocks. The Truth is beyond what appears as a material world."

The woman nodded "yes."

Sunny was amazed at her understanding of the concept. Sunny added that "The good book is telling you and me to start seeing the world differently. In spiritual terms. The woman agreed. For a moment Sunny felt on the same level as this upper class woman.

Another time while cleaning the woman's house, they discussed *The Lord's Prayer*. Sunny said, "I sometimes meditate on 'Thy Kingdom Come.' To me, 'Thy Kingdom Come' means to see the world with new eyes.'"

The woman said, "Yes, seeing the Kingdom of God with new eyes is so much hard work."

Sunny said, "Yes, because it is work to see the good in the world. To see ain't easy to see at times. No Sir, there is plenty of bad. To practice seeing 'Thy Kingdom Come' with new eyes brings me a better picture of God's good world. To see the Truth shining through the bad world. It makes my day happy instead of commonplace."

Her employer said Sunny was a wise woman.

Sometimes Sunny's employers would tell her about the conflicts they had with a neighbor or co-worker. Sunny told them, "You have to change your thinking about those folks. You must be willing to find the good in these folks; then hold to this view despite what's going on."

If the employer was open to more, Sunny turned to where the Bible says that God made each of us "very good." Sunny invoked that "By finding what is good, you will uncover a solution. The Bible tells us that the spiritual good creation is written in Genesis Chapter One. In Genesis Chapter Two is the Adam and Eve story of the physical creation.

"The revelation for us is that the Chapter One creation is spiritual and good and the physical creation in Chapter Two is a mess. We're in the physical creation. We are here to work out our problems by drawing on the truth from the spiritual creation which is all good."

Not bad insights coming from a woman with a fourth grade education.

Often there were arguments in the homes which Sunny overheard while she was cleaning. One time when a husband and wife were arguing over the price they'd paid for their new carpeting, each declared they'd paid a different amount. Their voices got shriller.

Sunny said to them, "Folks, it's not who's right, it's what's right." Sunny suggested, "You need to get the right amount from your check book." Sure enough, the price was there in the check book.

Sunny sweetened the atmosphere of many a home by her "what's right, not who's right" rule. Sunny said, **"When you push for who's right, that's heat, not light."**

When employers and friends asked how do you trust, Sunny expounded. Trust is not a blind faith. It means to trust God, to turn to Him in all your needs. I'm accustomed to trusting God with decisions. It took me a long time to listen to what God was telling me instead of telling God what I planned. I like the Proverb "Trust in the Lord with all thine heart; and lean not unto thine own understanding. In all thy ways acknowledge him, and he shall direct thy paths." (Prov. 3:5, 6)

An example of trust Sunny liked was the experience of a Christian Science practitioner when the practitioner was raising her family. This Chicago mother followed a tradition of sharing May Day baskets of flowers. On the first day of May, some families with a need or a sick person had a surprise knock on their door early in the morning. The children would knock on the door, leave a May basket, and run away before they were seen.

The tradition became an embarrassment when her son reached a certain age. He and his older sister decided it looked silly to be carrying baskets of flowers to the neighbors. It was a family decision not to make May Day baskets anymore.

The younger daughter felt left out. It appeared the feelings of the youngest weren't considered. So her mother told her younger daughter that the next May Day would be a special May Day.

April 30th arrived, but the May Day flowers had slipped the mother's mind. The mother went to bed. Her daughter came in the room crying, "What about the May Day flowers?" The mother thought she still had time.

She found some rolls of wallpaper. The daughter and mother made baskets with them. Her daughter said, "Where are the flowers?" The mother thought she could make some out of other paper, but she had none. The daughter went to bed.

The mother went in the living room to ponder and pray. She noted it was midnight when a car drove up the driveway. It was a friend who was returning from visiting relatives in the same town where her mother lived. Her friend and her husband had driven hundreds of miles and decided to stop at that late hour. The friend's arms were filled with lilacs from her mother.

In the morning the younger daughter was delighted with the lilacs. This experience was unanticipated and showed that we can trust God to figure out all the details when we can't.

Sunny mentioned a phrase that strengthened her trust. "Go into the darkness and put your hand in the hand of God. That shall be to you better than light and safer than a known way!" These words made Sunny feel that she could trust God for her well-being.

When discussing her work as a cleaning woman, Sunny said, "Mrs. Thompson was the most unhappy woman I worked for. She had a beautiful home, a good husband, and two lovely children. She followed me from room to room complaining. She never could abide the way I cleaned her refrigerator. I just did not put the food back in the exact same place. She never failed to fuss.

"I just couldn't take any more of her gloomy chatter. I burst out, 'Mrs. Thompson, you're the most grumpy person I ever met. You have the choice to choose happy thoughts or complaining thoughts.'

"Mrs. Thompson was shocked. She said, 'Sunny, I had no idea this is how I appear.' Mrs. Thomson walked out of the room. She never followed me around again and didn't complain too much."

CHAPTER SIXTEEN

SUNSHINE AND STORM

"A merry heart doeth good like medicine."
Proverbs 17:22

"Character not circumstances make the man."
Booker T. Washington

"There are three ingredients into the good life:
learning, earning, and yearning."
Christopher Morley

Sunny Looked Forward to the days she worked for Nelson Booth. Nelson Booth lived in Kenilworth next to Wilmette. Nelson was a bachelor who lived in a mansion on Sheridan Road overlooking Lake Michigan. The entire upper third floor was a ballroom. He had lots of friends and gave parties on Thanksgiving, Christmas, and Easter. He also held fundraisers for favorite charities. Mr. Booth had a huge pipe organ in the ballroom. On the first floor in the music room, he had a gold and green grand piano. The piano had flowers painted on it.

Nelson was brought up in Belington, West Virginia. Nelson came to Chicago when he was 17 years old. He worked as a helper in a fur salon. Now he owned the swankiest fur salon on State Street.

Nelson was accomplished as a musician. He played many instruments. He often played the piano and sang the official version of the West Virginia State Song, "The West Virginia Hills."

> Oh, the West Virginia Hills!
> How majestic and how grand,
> With their summits bathed in glory,
> Like our Prince Immanuel's Land!
> Is it any wonder then,
> That my heart with rapture thrills,
> As I stand once more with loved ones
> On those West Virginia hills?
>
> Oh, the West Virginia hills!
> Where my childhood hours were passed,
> Where I often wandered lonely,
> And the future tried to cast:
> Many are our visions bright,
> Which the future ne're fulfills:
> But how sunny were my day-dreams
> On those West Virginia hills!

Nelson was a natural baritone. He sang with such feeling that when he came to singing about his loved ones, Sunny had a hard time not crying. When Nelson had guests, he liked Sunny to sing her spirituals in her high soprano voice.

After knowing her for some time, Nelson gave Sunny a mink stole. It was fashionable then to leave the head, legs, and tails on the body of the minks. Hers was lined with a lovely, soft, brown satin. In the fall and early spring, Sunny wore it proudly each Sunday to church.

Even after Sunny no longer did day work, Nelson would visit her at her home and bring her fruit and flowers with a check inside the wrappings.

Sunny liked to help Diana Swanson with the Academy Award party she held for friends every year on Oscar night. The individual tables had a plastic $12.50 Oscar in the center. Each guest came dressed as her favorite movie star. Diana wanted Sunny to come as a movie star, too. When Sunny said she was going to come as Hattie Daniels, Diana said, "I suggest you come as the glamorous Lena Horn and win the best music award. Could you sing some of Lena's songs for us?" Sunny said, "Sure." She came as Lena Horn. She did sing and won the music award. Sunny had a place to sit at one of the tables. She felt like she was one of the suburban North Shore guests, and she was.

Twice a month Sunny cleaned the home of a blind lady in Evanston. Most people just change their sheets and put on clean ones every week. Ms. Findle had Sunny change her sheets every two weeks. Sunny scrubbed the cat's dishes and pan. She put in clean litter and sprayed the upstairs and downstairs with disinfectant spray. The cat followed Ms. Findle, sat on her lap and slept in her bed.

Ms. Findle had been a professional pianist and organist. She told Sunny it was less expensive for her to hire someone to stay with her and maintain her home than to live in a nursing home. Besides she could play her grand piano at all hours and play with her cat. Friends from her church came by to read religious articles to her. She also listened to hymns and religious articles on her tape recorder. Working for Ms. Findle was not pleasant like working in her other homes. The way Ms. Findle spoke to Sunny when she ordered Sunny around made Sunny unhappy. The day the colored man who was taking care of the lawn came to the door and asked to use the rest room was the last day Sunny worked for Ms. Findle.

Ms. Findle said, "No, you cannot come in the house. There is a gas station about three blocks away."

Sunny thought that this blind lady was blind to the meaning of what her church friends were reading to her from the Bible and religious magazines.

Sunny recalled a strange experience when doing housework for the Jensens in Northbrook. She knew their son was fighting in Vietnam. Sunny was told later that both Mr. and Mrs. Jensen both had the same dream during the night. They saw their son in full uniform saying, "I'm all right. Don't worry about me." The son waved and walked away.

The next morning, Mr. and Mrs. Jensen didn't tell each other about the dreams they had. A military car drove into their driveway. Three soldiers got out and informed the Jensens that their son had been killed. Sunny thanked God for placing her at their home when they received the information. Sunny spoke softly and gave them some comfort.

Two weeks later, Sunny suggested that Mr. and Mrs. Jensen read pages 116 and 117 in *J. B. Phillips'* book *The Ring of Truth*. The book tells of a respected theologian, C. S. Lewis, who had contact with Mr. Phillips after Lewis had passed on. Sunny didn't know if the Jensens followed her suggestion until months later when Mrs. Jensen thanked Sunny for mentioning the book.

At a later date, Sunny told the Jensens, "Jesus said, 'I will see you again, and your heart shall rejoice.'" (John 16: 22) Sunny continued, "Nothing can separate you from those you love. In your material state, you can no longer speak to your son, but he can speak to you through your consciousness. Your son knows death as nothing but a fence about life here. He has gone forward to a clearer understanding of life with all its activity, peace, and joy. You will see your loved one again, and what appears to mortal sense to be final, you will understand as an illusion as a fence.

CHAPTER SEVENTEEN

OUTRAGEOUS

"What we need . . . is not division . . . is not hatred . . .
not violence, but love and wisdom and compassion."
Robert F. Kennedy

"A beautiful behavior is better than a beautiful form."
Ralph Waldo Emerson

"I am still determined to be cheerful and happy in whatever
situation I may be, for I have also learned from experience that
the greatest part of our happiness or misery depends on
our own dispositions and not on our circumstances."
Martha Washington

Sunny Knew How to rent rooms. The third floor of
Sunny's Wilmette home had been an attic. Mr. Rogal
made it into an apartment. She had two rooms, a hall, and a bath
put in. He charged Sunny nine hundred dollars. On the second
floor she had two rooms, a kitchen, and bath. She got thirty-five

dollars a week for the second floor apartment and twenty a week for the third floor apartment. On the first floor, Mrs. Brown paid fifteen a week for the room off the dining room. The baby she cared for brought Sunny thirty-five dollars a week.

Sunny said proudly, "I'm not high on the hog, but I've got eight hundred dollars in the bank. I will pay five hundred dollars out of it for the carpeting upstairs."

Sunny purchased carpeting at a reasonable price for her front room and dining room. It was turquoise carpeting. Turquoise carpeting was a popular color in 1965. It went wall to wall.

Sunny could not get anything she needed on time. She also had to pay cash for everything. It seems after you get a certain age, banks don't loan you money. When she first moved to Wilmette, Sunny borrowed twelve hundred dollars from Halstead Street Bank. That's where she got the five hundred dollars to pay the carpenter, Mr. Rogel.

Sunny went to her job at seven in the morning. She stood on the corner waiting for the bus. She worked all day until five o'clock. When Sunny got off the bus at night, instead of going home, she'd go to someone else's home. She cooked their dinner and cleaned the dishes. They sometimes wanted her to sit with the children until eleven o'clock.

Buck was lazy. Buck wanted to dress like a dandy and be the mister, but Sunny had to do the work around the house and bring in the money. When the leaves fell, Sunny's husband, Buck, wouldn't help her rake the leaves.

Sunny bought bushes to be planted on the west side of the house. The bushes came with a burlap bag tied around their roots. When she left for work, she said, "Buck, I expect you to plant the bushes while I'm gone."

Buck looked up from reading the morning paper, saying, "I won't do it! I ain't got no work clothes to do dirty work. I can't get my clothes filled with dirt."

"Sunny replied, "I don't care what you wear. Wear your pajamas. They can be washed. You plant those bushes, Buck"

Buck laughed.

When Sunny came home from work, she went to the west side of the house to see her bushes. They were just as the man from the greenhouse left them. She went in the house, and there was Buck stretched out on the sofa listening to the radio a woman she worked for had given her.

As Sunny made dinner, she preached to Buck about how lazy, self-centered, and unreliable he was. Turning to Buck after dinner, she warned, "This is the last meal I'm fixing for you until you plant those bushes. You expect me to work all day and then come home and plant those bushes. Well, this time I'm not going to plant no bushes. You're going to plant them or you're not going to eat the food I buy."

Buck laughed. He got all dolled up in his best clothes and walked out the door. Sunny never did know where he went, but this time when he asked for money, she wouldn't give it to him. She kept thinking how hard it is to be married to a lady's man and keep the wedding vow "till death do us part." The Saints told her not to marry that man, but she didn't listen so now she was paying for her bad decision.

The next evening Buck had not planted the bushes. Sunny said not a word but fixed herself a meal from leftovers. She made sure there was no food in the house and went about as usual. Buck could not believe she made no dinner for him.

By the next evening when Sunny came home, the bushes were all planted. During the following weeks, instead of growing bigger and bigger, the bushes turned yellow and died. She went to the manager of the greenhouse.

He said, "Those are the hardiest bushes there are. The only reason they would not grow is because the dumbbell who planted them did not remove the burlap bag around the roots."

When Sunny dug up the bushes, there were the burlap bags still around the roots. She thought, "That man just don't have common sense. I have to do everything myself. Buck is only good at pressing his clothes and looking like a dandy."

Buck wasn't a husband to Sunny. Sunny fixed a separate bedroom for him. They didn't sleep together for twenty-seven years. Buck ran around with other women during that time. Buck stayed out late at night. Sunny never knew what he was doing. She never tried to find out, even though it bothered her.

Sunny furnished the money for everything. Buck didn't make any money. She gave him money to shop downtown, to have whatever he wanted done, like his shoes fixed, his hair cut. He pressed *his own* clothes because he'd been a presser and did it better than Sunny. That's all he did. He pressed his own clothes and kept himself looking like a million.

Buck said he was going to take a group out that would vote for him to get a job. He'd take these people out, but they didn't vote for him and get him a job. Sunny quit giving him money when he came up with that particular story. Sunny paid the rent, the light bill, the telephone bill, the gas bill, and bought the food. She made the vow for better or for worse, which was surely for richer or poorer.

Buck's sisters passed on before Sunny bought her home in Wilmette. When Sunny had that fight with Pearl, they took Buck to Mississippi with them. He stayed two years. Then Buck begged Sunny to let him come back. But Sunny never slept with him from then on. Occasionally the Saints reminded Sunny he wouldn't be a good husband because he wasn't saved. When Sunny met Buck, he was active in his church. But that was no guarantee that he was saved.

Sunny told Miss Lindsey to choose a saved man when she brought her date from the south side to visit. Later, Sunny asked if he was a saved man.

"No, but he said he'd get saved," Miss Lindsey answered.

Sunny shook her finger. "Saved nothing! If you ask me, all he wants is to get to you, and then he'll do just as he wants!"

Events showed Sunny was right.

THE WAY WE ARE

When Sunny fixed dinners at her home in Wilmette, she put an extra place setting on the table. She never would say why she performed this ritual. Friends thought the ritual was strange but kept their mouths shut. They always felt an unseen presence was at the table. One day Sunny hinted that the place setting was for a dear relative.

As the adage goes, Buck Buchanan entered in a conversation for nothing but to brag. One of Buck's old friends came from the south side to visit.

He said, "Buck Buchanan, how did you get out here to Wilmette?"

Buck stuck his fingers in his vest, "My money put me out here."

When the friend left, Sunny said, "Buck, don't tell anybody that again. If you tell anybody that again before me, I'm going to make you ashamed. It was my money. I sacrificed and made the money for this home. I put my money in the First National Bank. I gave you a key, so when you made money, you could go put money in the Bank. But did you? No!"

Sunny recalled the past. When they were living in Chicago, Buck worked at the bank across the street from the First National Bank. Sunny asked Buck, "I gotta have that key. You don't need it. You don't go down there and put money in. Give me my key."

"I will not. I won't give you nothing," Buck retorted.

Sunny went to the bank and changed the keys. Sunny fixed it so he couldn't get anything out.

Every week Sunny worked she put a little money in an envelope with the date, sealed the envelope, and put it in the box. She had over $500 in the box.

When Buck was working at the bank, he bought a liberty loan for 83 dollars. When he was working on the railroad, he came in with his check for 65 dollars. The rent was 75 dollars. There were the furniture bills, the grocery bills, and other bills.

Sometimes Buck would hide his money. The Spirit would send Sunny right to the place to find it. She would take it and not say a word. He'd come in and look and look.

Sunny would say, "What you looking for?"

"Oh, I'm just looking for something."

Sunny knew what he was looking for. He hid money in the chifforobe under the papers. The Spirit of the Lord told Sunny where it was.

Sunny bought the Wilmette home thinking she'd have a fine place for her mama, Em, but Mama wouldn't live with Sunny.

She told her mama, "Mama, you don't have no tin bucket or nothing. I have two bathrooms downstairs and one on second and one on third. I've got everything that you need. What do you want to see?"

"Sunny, you got too many white folks. I don't want to see white folks. I want to see Negroes."

No matter what was appealing about Wilmette, Sunny never got her mama to live with her.

When Sunny first moved to Wilmette, a black family rented the living quarters upstairs. A man and wife and two children. Sunny told them they couldn't bring a dog in her house. But they did. Her front door was made of plate glass like they have in stores. He'd let the dog out. The dog would come back and jump on that door. So the door was muddy and nasty all the time.

Sunny scolded, "Mr. Larson, I asked you not to have a dog. You let him out to go free instead of taking him out on a leash. He comes back and messes my door. I can't have that. I didn't want to keep you, but you couldn't get any place because you had children. I kept you."

Mr. Larson said, "I pay you rent."

Sunny responded, "The 27 dollars a month you pay isn't enough money for a five room place upstairs. When I moved here, upstairs was open from the front to the back. I put a lot of money to fix up your place."

Mr. Larson's wife was a nice person. He was a bully and was noisy. At night he'd beat his drum until ten or eleven and blow his horn. Sunny and Buck could hardly sleep.

Sunny said to him, "Mr. Larson, you should allow us to have some rest down here. What do you think this is? A band house?"

He said, "I got to practice."

Sunny sternly, "Go where you have a place to practice. This is not the place."

When Sunny couldn't take anymore, she asked Mr. Larson to move. Mr. Larson told her he wasn't going to move. He would like to see her try to put him out. She went down to the city hall and reported he did not cooperate. Sunny got a warrant, a five-day notice. City Hall told her to give him the five-day notice. After Sunny gave Mr. Larson the notice, he got a lawyer and fought it. Sunny got a lawyer.

Sunny was 58 years old then, and Buck was seven years older, 65. When neither lawyer could make any headway, Sunny's lawyer told Mr. Larson, "The Buchanans are at the age now that they need a quiet home. They are working to have a home. You don't cooperate with them. You make too much trouble. You're a young man. You should be working to try to make yourself a home. You've got two children to raise. These folks are entitled to their own home if they want it."

Sunny's lawyer told her to give Mr. Larson another five-day notice. He told her not to put it in his mail box, but to hand it to him. Sunny did. She went upstairs and told him, "Mr. Larson, here's a letter for you."

Sunny gave it to him. He read it.

He requested, "Give me five more days?"

Sunny acquiesced, "Four or five days you're going to get out."

Mr. Larson and his family got out. They left one piece of furniture. Mr. Larson took the pipe out of the flue, locked the door, and took the key with him.

Sunny told her husband, "Let's go upstairs and see how it looks. The Spirit keeps telling me to go see."

Sunny and Buck went upstairs. Everything was gone except a couch. Suddenly Sunny heard a roaring sound. She looked up. When the furnace went on, a flame came out in the room. Mr. Larson had pulled the pipe out of the wall that went into the chimney. If a wind had blown, Sunny would have been burned out. She affirmed that God kept her.

Buck said, "Sunny, you the uncanniest person I've ever known. Nothing gits by you."

Sunny had a hard time with Mr. Larson. She said, "God kept me going. If He hadn't kept me going, we would have been burned out. Oh, dear God, how He did keep me. What a wonderful Savior I have."

Sunny said, "I ask God to protect me and see, He protects us. He throws his strong arms around us. What do you think if I didn't understand when the Spirit speaks?" Sunny sent word to Mr. Larson to get that trash out of the apartment. He never got it. Buck put the couch in the alley. Mr. Larson gave Sunny the worse name. He talked about her to the folks in Evanston. He told them what a mean person Sunny was. It didn't make any difference to Sunny. She prayed on.

Years later the doorbell rang. There was Mr. Larson with his two children and wife standing at the door. Sunny let them in and treated them nicely. She showed them how she built a nursery and added a new roof with gutters since they were there.

The Larsons bragged to her about all the improvements that had been done.

"The Lord made it possible," said Sunny.

Sunny never brought up how they acted. She carried on just as though it never happened. Mr. Larson still played in a band, but he worked in construction in the daytime.

After the Larsons had moved out of the apartment, Sunny let people stay who had just come up from the South. She rented rooms to many different people. The rent money helped to pay for her home. Some of these people took advantage of her. They'd bring in their friends and their in-laws and their outlaws. When she would come home after working all day, there would be extra people in the rooms. She'd go upstairs to see what was going on and say, "Who are you? Where you live at?" They always would be someone's cousin or relative.

"Well, they ain't got no business renting you no room up here. You ain't got no business staying here. I rent this place to a man and wife and no children."

Some renters would stay and wouldn't pay. Sometimes they'd move their whole families in. When the renters left, some of them would take Sunny's furniture. They moved her furniture out while she was working. She never knew what they did with her furniture.

Buck passed on in 1951. Sunny worked hard doing housework until 1962.

Butterfly Wings

Like a butterfly emerges
And unfolds its' graceful wings,
A child grows and develops
With the love a mother brings.
I'm thankful for the times
When you encouraged me to try,
For God gave me my wings,
But, Mom, you taught me how to fly.

Author - Robin Fogle

CHAPTER EIGHTEEN

THE NURSERY

"To labor is to pray."
St. Benedict

"Anything you're good at contributes to happiness."
Bertrand Russell

"Get a good idea and stay with it. Dog it,
and work at it until it's done, and done right."
Walt Disney

After Selling Their home in Glencoe, Mr. and Mrs. Chapman moved in with Sunny. They took the first floor room off the dining room. That was Sunny's husband's room before he passed on. Mrs. Chapman didn't do anything but stay in her room all day. She read all day. When her husband came home, he took her out to dinner.

Mr. Chapman was the nicest man. Sunny rented the garage to him for $4 a month. Sunny worked outside of her home until 1962. Then Sunny did some thinking. She thought she'd have to work at home, or she'd have no home. Her renters would move out her stuff and move in their folks. She asked the Lord what she should do. Prayer confirmed to her to stay home. She talked it over with Mrs. Chapman. They were good friends. Mrs. Chapman made them both a cup of tea.

Sunny said, "I heard you say there was a nursery next door to your daughter. I wonder if I could open up a nursery?"

Mrs. Chapman said, "Yes, there is a nursery next to my daughter's place."

Sunny said, "Next time she calls, you ask her how do you go about starting a nursery?"

Mrs. Chapman's daughter called Sunny and said a nursery required a permit from Springfield. Sunny went to the Wilmette City Hall, and an arrangement was begun with them. As she was walking up the stairs, she met the building commissioner, Mr. Daniels.

Sunny said, "Good morning."

Mr. Daniels said, "Good morning. Can I help you?"

Sunny replied, "Yes, if you're willing. I want to open up a nursery. My husband died in '51. So much is going on around my home, I can't keep up with it and work outside too."

Mr. Daniels asked, "What kind of nursery?"

Sunny answered, "I sit with children every day, but sometimes two people call me for the same day. I can't go out to two different places. If I had a nursery in my home, I could take them both in one day. I was told to see you about a local permit."

Mr. Daniels said helpfully, "My secretary is upstairs. You go and talk to her. She'll tell you what to do."

When Sunny went upstairs, the secretary said, "We'll have to send a letter to Springfield for the permit. It takes about two weeks before we hear from them."

When Sunny went home, she prayed, "Lord, you know I need to stay in my home. Make a way where I can take children in my own home and won't have to go out and do day work no more."

After two weeks Sunny went back and again met commissioner Daniels coming down the stairs. She said, "Did the permit come?"

Mr. Daniels said, "I don't know, Mrs. Buchanan. Ask my secretary.

The secretary greeted her and replied, "No permit has come. My boss went out for a few minutes for coffee break. You can talk with him."

Sunny waited. When commissioner Daniels came back, he asked, "Well, are you teaching children?"

Sunny shook her head, "No, sir, I'm not teaching children. I'm sitting with children. Just like you want me to come to your house and sit with your child while your wife goes out. Somebody else calls me. I can go to only one place. If I can have a nursery in my home, I can take care of more than one child at a time."

Mr. Daniels asked, "How much do you charge?"

Mrs. Buchanan answered, "People pay me different prices. Some pay one dollar an hour. Some fifty cents an hour. I get fifty cents an hour when I do day work. If I was home with some children, that would save me from having to go out."

Mr. Daniels said, "Mrs. Buchanan, I thought you were going to have a school."

Mrs. Buchanan affirmed, "No, I told you a nursery. I'm not a teacher. I just want to sit with children."

Mr. Daniels shrugged his shoulders, "Well, you got the green light. You don't have to have a permit. Go ahead."

Sunny Buchanan smiled, "Thank you. I don't want to do anything against the law."

Mr. Daniels smiled too and said, "I'm giving you permission. You can open up your home and take in children. I suggest you put an ad in the paper."

Mrs. Buchanan asserted, "Yes, I'll put an ad in the *Wilmette Life*, the town's weekly paper."

Sunny walked to the *Wilmette Life* building. She knew a friend there from church. Sunny told her she wanted to open a nursery for working and shopping mothers. She could care for them by the hour, by the week, by the day or night. She had room upstairs where children could sleep. Sunny's friend wrote out an advertisement.

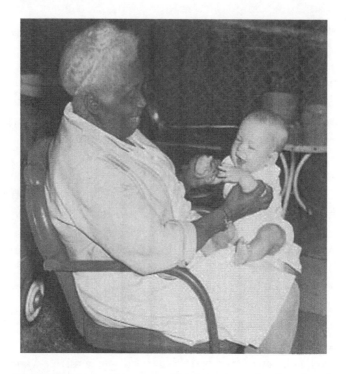

The friend later recommended Sunny to a husband and wife who had just arrived from Holland. They had a little boy, Johnny. The couple hired Sunny to care for Johnny. They brought their baby to Mrs. Buchanan at 7:30 in the morning. Johnny came in smiling and left smiling. Johnny's mother brought his food. She was a cosmetic woman in Europe. Old Orchard Shopping Center didn't pay her enough, so she got a job working as a cosmetic consultant at the Marshall Fields store in Chicago's Loop. Johnny was eighteen months old.

Later Johnny stayed with Sunny after school until his father picked him up. Johnny's mother told Sunny that the teacher said he had a learning problem. Sunny reacted, "That can't be. God created Johnny in His likeness. God doesn't have a learning problem, and Johnny is His likeness. Now that's what's true about your son."

Sunny told Johnny to listen to his teacher, and even if the work was too hard to do to keep trying. The next year Johnny had a teacher who didn't see he had a learning problem. Johnny became a good student.

Johnny went into the army after high school. He told Sunny goodbye before leaving for Vietnam. Sunny told him, "God will protect you. Remember the words from the 46th Psalm: 'God shall help you, and that right early.'"

Johnny was promoted to Sergeant. A picture of Johnny in uniform was prominent in Sunny's house. When his tour of duty was over, he told Sunny, "I owe my life to you. When my men were on patrol, we walked into an ambush. The Viet Cong soldiers killed some of my men, and we were all in peril. I saw the Viet Cong go through the pockets of my downed men. I saw the Cong look at me, but they didn't see me. I thought of your prayers for me. Suddenly the Cong left. We found our way back to my battalion."

Sunny teared up, "Yes, each time I thought of you during the day or night, I prayed that Johnny be protected and be invisible to the enemy. You were invisible."

Johnny became a master electrician and owned his own business. He never forgot Sunny on holidays.

Sunny was delighted that people answered her ad. One lady brought her little girl while they flew to Denver for ten days to ski. Becky was four years old. She just loved Sunny's cat. Becky squeezed the cat so hard that the cat screeched. Sunny corrected Becky, "A good girl wouldn't do that, and you're a good girl." Sunny showed Becky how to treat a cat by petting it gently. Sunny taught children how to behave. They paid Sunny $110 for caring for their little girl. On some days Sunny made $50. Some mothers had Sunny care for their children while they went to the Loop for a whole day. Others would drop their children off at six o'clock in the evening and come for their children at eleven o'clock. The parents played that game of *Twirling* on the ice. Sunny put the children in bed. They would sleep until their parents came to pick them up. The parents paid Sunny one dollar an hour. Sometimes she had five to ten children at the same time. She kept a book with the names and addresses of her customers and the amount of money she received. She paid for her mortgage with the money.

When Sunny needed to go to the store, Mrs. Chapman would take care of the children. When Sunny didn't have any children at night, she'd go out and serve parties and wash dishes. Sunny worked like a horse.

Sunny planned an open house. She placed an ad in the *Wilmette Life*. She put a sign in her window later. For the open house, she invited the Board of Health, the Fire Department, the Police Department, and the Nurse Department. The inspectors came and looked over her house. It passed inspection. In 1971, Wilmette made a rule that you couldn't put an ad in a window.

Some white school teachers on Elm Street got together and bought a station wagon to take children to the beach. They saw Sunny's children in her back yard and thought they would start a nursery and take the children to the lake.

Sunny met a lady at the post office. She said, "You have big competition now since these three teachers bought a station wagon and are taking children to the lake."

"Well," Sunny said, "Marshall Fields didn't shut down because Carson Pirie Scott opened up next door to them. What's for me, I'll get. I hope what's for them they'll get. I'm not really worried. God bless them!

Sunny had a wood fence between her yard and the park. The three teachers brought the children from the lake to the park to play. The children liked to climb up on the fence and walk from the garage to the front. They broke down the fence. She never did get acquainted with the teachers. The teachers said they were going to have her care for some of their children. They never did. They just wanted to find out her prices and how Sunny ran her business. Sunny told them. She would not lie. She got fifty cents an hour for some of them. Sunny never did know what happened to the teachers with the station wagon. After their children broke the fence down, they never came back to the park with the children.

Sunny cared for children from all the suburbs on the North Shore: Wilmette, Kenilworth, Northbrook, Winnetka, Northfield, and all the way to Glencoe. She had children from Evanston, too. Sunny had two ice boxes on her second floor where she kept little containers of milk, cookies, and apples. Before she put the children to sleep, she would give them milk and cookies. Some mothers had Sunny care for two of their children. She charged $1.50 an hour because that was two times the work.

Sunny often observed, "Caring for children is tough work. Some of the children aren't raised right. They just run all over their mothers. These mothers were just too lenient. It's easy to let kids do what they want."

One mother asked Sunny for advice. Sunny gave her opinion. "Mothers don't want to be mothers no more. Mothers that love their children correct them and make them do what is right. I'm starting to hear the same with teachers. They just sit with students. They let the children write anything they want to and don't correct the spelling. Some teachers let them choose what they want to do, so they become self confident and happy. They let them swear, too. That's no way to achieve that, I hear. But school principals don't enforce the rules either. I sense the change in the way kids are taught. It ain't like when I was in school."

Generally speaking the North Shore people spoke the King's perfect English. Most residents believed swear words were wrong to speak and showed people who swore were ignorant.

Sunny thought using swear words was a sin. Sunny believed that words had the power to bring ill will or happiness into her home. She said, "When you murder, you kill *one* person. When you swear, you contaminate *everyone* who hears your voice." Sunny permitted no foul language by children or their parents. She often quoted, "Kind words are like dripping honey, sweetness on the tongue and health for the body." (Proverbs 16: 24 *New English Bible*)

Sunny said that preachers should take seriously the damage that bad language was doing to the people in our country. Cursing is mentioned as a sin in the *Ten Commandments*. This third commandant is the only one that states a threat to mankind if it's disobeyed. "You shall not take the name of the Lord your God in vain; for the Lord will not hold him guiltless who takes His name in vain." (Exodus 20:7)

Cursing was bad enough in ancient Bible times to sometimes lead to capital punishment by stoning. Sunny mentioned to a parent the first of the nine stonings in the Bible. An Israelite mother and an Egyptian father had a son who went out among the children of Israel. The son blasphemed the name of the Lord and cursed constantly annoying many people. "Moses spoke to the children of Israel, that they should bring forth him that had cursed out of the camp and stone him with stones. And the children did as the Lord commanded Moses." (Leviticus 24:10-23) The parent was shocked by that Bible story.

The nursery got so active that, when Sunny was busy, the children would go in the ice box and grab an apple. They'd take one bite and then not eat anymore. Then nobody else wanted the apple.

She told their mothers, "If you want your child to have an apple, you bring it with him. Bring their milk, too. I won't furnish no more cookies and apples. I'm not cutting the price. It isn't any play keeping children. It's real work."

Sunny had to lock doors. She put catches over the bathroom door. They liked to play in the water in the toilet. After they played and hour and a half outdoors, Sunny would say, "Anybody want to go upstairs to the bathroom?"

Only one or two wanted to go. When she came back down, they'd say, "I want to go to the toilet."

She'd have to go up the steps with them. That was too much walking up the steps for Sunny. It almost broke her down. Sunny prayed about it. The Lord told her to build a nursery on the back of her house.

Mrs. Nelson lived next door. She was a smart woman. She taught part-time at the Wilmette schools. Mrs. Nelson brought fresh bread she'd baked and jelly to Sunny almost every week.

She came in one day, "Mrs. Buchanan, my husband is going to California for six weeks. I'm going with him."

While they were gone, Sunny prayed about the nursery. She went down to the city hall and told the man what she wanted to do.

He asked, "If you don't have a contractor, I'll send a contractor to see you."

Sunny told the contractor what she wanted, "I want a big room from the kitchen door out to the back. Also a bathroom next to it."

When the carpenter started putting in windows on the side by the Nelsons, the spirit told Sunny not to because they would be able to see what she was doing. It would be more private for her to have one side with no windows and the other sides all windows. That's the way Sunny planned her nursery.

When the Nelsons came back, the foundation was dug out for the nursery, and the workmen were putting in the concrete. The Nelsons thought what Sunny was doing was terrible. It cut off the view from their house. Sunny was concerned that the Nelsons would be upset with her. When the nursery was finished, the Nelsons wouldn't come in and see it. It took three years before they spoke to Sunny. Mr. Nelson finally brought Sunny a carton of homemade jelly. Sunny was relieved.

CELEBRATION

Sunny held a barbecue in her back yard, to celebrate the completion of the nursery. Her friends wondered why there were so many butterflies.

Sunny quipped, "Butterflies seem to know they bring me peace so they come around my back yard."

The Nelson's didn't come. Friends came from the South side of Chicago and from the North Shore suburbs including Wilmette. Sunny had the food on a long table inside the nursery. The nursery had windows overlooking the back yard. Two barbecue cookers were outside the nursery's windows. On one barbecue were chickens. On the other hamburgers and wieners.

The day prior Sunny prepared baked beans. Most of her friends knew about Sunny's baked beans. They were legendary.

Sunny's Baked Beans

1 64 oz. can of beans
5 big onions
1 cup of brown sugar
2 T dry mustard
1/2 bottle of catsup
1/2 lb. of fried bacon (cut in 1" pieces)
Drain off 3/4 to 1/2 of the fat.
Fry onions in bacon fat.
Combine all ingredients.
Coat the top with brown sugar.
Bake at 300 degrees temperature for 3 hours.

Optional 2 T of sorghum

Sunny had friends from Mississippi that sent her 2 quarts of sorghum every fall

*   *   *

On the day of the barbecue, Sunny made bowls of her delicious fruit salad.

Sunny's Fruit Salad

2 cans Mandarin oranges drained
2 cans Geisha tropical fruit
1 can sliced peaches drained
1 can tid-bit pineapple drained
Add bananas or any other fruit.
1 cup or more sour cream
1 cup small marshmallows or more

1 scant cup coconut flakes
Bind the sour cream, marshmallows,
coconut together. Mix over fruit.
Cover and let set in the refrigerator for 3 hours.
Serve.

Sunny rented tables and chairs. At twilight the group sang all the old familiar songs so dear to their hearts. It was a memorable feeling bringing some of the old South to the North Shore of Chicago. Sunny's neighbors, including the Nelsons, were nervous about the party. That was because it was the first one she'd done in Wilmette

CHAPTER NINETEEN

BLESSINGS

"No act of kindness, no matter how small, is ever wasted."
Aesop, *The Lion and the Mouse*

"He who wants to do good knocks on the gate;
he who loves finds the gate open."
Rabindra

"Do little things now; so shall big things come
to thee by and by asking to be done."
Persian Proverb

S unny Had No car. Amy Anderson lived two doors west
of Sunny's home. When Amy went to Old Orchard or
Edens Plaza shopping centers to shop, she invited Sunny to come
with her. Amy liked the conversations they had together. Amy
was skeptical when Sunny talked of her trust in God. She confided
that she didn't go to church to learn more about God. She went
to church for the social activities.

Sunny told Amy that whenever she found something helpful, she continued to study each word until the ideas became a part of her thinking. Sunny said, "I have no idea where I heard this or read this, but I memorized it, and here is what I think each morning:"

I know there is only one Mind.
Mind is God. *This day* is the unfoldment of
God's plan.
Because my intelligence comes to me from
Mind (God)'
I have unseen intelligence to draw on.

Amy felt God changed His Mind all the time, sometimes leaving man to suffer on his own. It's understandable considering what you see. Beyond what you see are God's facts.

Amy questioned Sunny. "How can I believe other than from what I see?"

Sunny answered, "God don't change, honey. The change is in us. It is in the mind, then in our acting. We are sometimes lambasted and look like we're mistreated, but that's all right. Jesus was treated in a bad way, too. They spit on him and called him Beelzebub, one of Satan's devils. Imagine that. Jesus, a devil. But was that the truth? No."

After a pause Amy wanted to hear more. Sunny continued, "We have to walk in Jesus' footprints if we are following him. I rejoice saying, 'Thank you Father'. I'm not alone. God is with me and gives me what I need. With the Lord you don't have to talk out loud. You just think it out loud. He's been so wonderful with my situation. Like I told my husband. God is my banker. All the moneys says 'In God We Trust.' I trust God for what I get. Money is in His bank, isn't it? That's the source of money."

Amy, began to get it and said, "Then that Mind can be the source of my money, too."

Sunny replied, "Yes, Amy. You see, I give money. I pay my tithes every Sunday. A tenth you know. Then God blesses me.

Tithes is paying a dime out of every dollar that you make. You read that in Malachi. Sometimes the Lord puts it on me to give more money lovingly. Because my Father is rich. Things I need He gives me in return.

Sunny repeated an experience with money. "Today is Leap Year. On February 29, 1972, I paid out $1,755.99. The money went for a new power line from the alley up to the third floor to operate a heater for my tenant.

Yesterday God started increasing my money in the bank. Jimmy's parents were paying me $6 each day they brought in the baby. Now they pay me in advance. Each Monday they give me $42."

Sunny preached, "Oh, yes, I can trust God. He is my advertiser. I tell my Father what I want and hope it properly fits His will. I always say, 'If you *will* it. Thy *will* be done.'"

BUSY WILMETTE DAYS

While living in Wilmette, Sunny sometimes spent happy hours fishing in a lagoon. Someone from her church would drive her to her favorite spot near Skokie Lagoon and pick her up. She liked being alone sitting in the soft grass by the little brook which ran close to the highway. Sunny prized her store bought fishing pole. It mattered not if she caught any fish. She was awed by the trees, the brook, the sky, the environment around her, and the good thoughts which came to her as she fished. Fishing has a spiritual effect on some people and Sunny was one. Sunny knew some vegetarians who felt fishing was killing life and wasn't spiritual at all. It goes to show good people can have different opinions about fishing.

While fishing Sunny thought back to when she lived in Chicago and belonged to the Sanctified Church. She recalled In Acts, chapters I, II, and III and in St. John, the Bible says to sanctify yourself, which means to practice what you believe.

Peter prayed for the people to be sanctified and receive the Holy Ghost. "And they were all filled with the Holy Ghost."

Acts 2:4 First John, Second John, Third John are all the letters
of the school of St. John.

Jesus talks to the people:

> Sanctify them through the truth; thy word is truth.
> Thou hast sent me into the world. Even so have I
> sent them [his disciples] into the world. For their
> sakes I sanctify myself, that they also may be
> sanctified through the truth. Neither pray I for
> these alone, but for them also who shall believe
> on me through their word; that they all may be
> one; as Thou Father, art in me, and I in thee, that
> they also may be one is us. ((John 17: 17-31,
> NKJV.)

When Sunny moved from Chicago to Wilmette, she began
going to the Christian Science church. She didn't choose to go to
the Baptist church. She was saved in the Baptist church, but she
never heard them say anything about sanctification. They didn't
teach it as far as she knew. The Christian Science people taught
sanctification and healing, too. Sunny said, "Sanctification is *acting*
like you are the image of God. Sanctification comes after you
become a believer in Jesus Christ and God. Then you are in the
same sanctification state. It's how you act, how you follow
through, with your works. It's like the preacher says, 'Being saved
is a matter of believing *and behaving*. Not believing alone.'"

Not Christian Scientists but most sanctified people taught
the Holy Dance. That is when the Spirit moves you to rejoice in
the Lord. You clap your hands and want to get out there and
praise the Lord, even shout. This is called the Holy Dance. In
Christian Science you do not have the Holy Dance, unfortunately.
Sunny missed the dancing.

The first time Sunny applied for membership in her Christian
Science church, the Board of Directors did not let her join. You
meet with the Board, and they decide if you understand the
teachings of Christian Science enough to join. You are asked to

give an explanation of Christ Jesus. Sunny aced that. Sunny also knew that the Christ idea is the spiritual man God created. Jesus was the human man that walked the earth. Together Christ and Jesus made Christ Jesus. She also seemed to know more about the Bible than anyone on the Board. She could quickly turn to any passage. The problem was she didn't yet know specific teachings of the denomination. She kept on studying and praying. When Sunny applied again, they accepted her. She would attend the church on Sunday. At the Wednesday meetings, she stood up and testified. The Christian Scientists did a whole lot more thinking than dancing.

While attending the Wilmette Church, Sunny was accepted for Class Instruction in Christian Science by a certified teacher. Class Instruction is a two week study of the Bible and the chapter on "Recapitulation" in the textbook *Science and Health with Key to the Scriptures* by Mary Baker Eddy. Sunny's teacher was highly qualified. Her teacher was chosen to go to Boston to teach a class of thirty Christian Science practitioners to become certified as teachers themselves.

Sunny told the teacher that since childhood, she wondered how God could hear billions of prayers at once. If a billion people were praying, for a billion different things, how did God hear all those prayers, let alone give a billion different answers?

During Class Instruction, Sunny learned that God answers prayers according to how they match up to spiritual laws. God's will is in harmony with His spiritual laws. When people petition God through prayer, if the petitions are within God's purpose for man, spiritual laws answer the prayers. Spiritual laws, like mathematical laws, are governed by a "higher principle." Sunny was delighted to know about the higher principle governing spiritual laws, because she wondered about these billions of prayers going to God all her life.

The teacher told Sunny that she herself was taught that the principle of mathematics helps to illustrate **"the principle of abundant prayer."** The teacher explained. "If a billion people applied the principle of mathematics to solve a problem, the principle would help each person to arrive at an individual solution the same way as if only one person were using that same principle. It's the same with our prayers. We can address our individual desires and prayers to the Divine Mind, God. Divine Mind is also Divine Principle. By submitting our prayers to Divine Principle, what will surface in life are good answers and resolutions to problems. God individualizes His answers to each of us as He answers individually the billions of prayers according to how these prayers *harmonize* with the spiritual laws of Principle."

Sunny thought to herself. "Since my childhood, a nagging question has been left in limbo until now. How could the world survive with billions and billions of people praying for different things to happen at once?" Sunny realized that if God answered a billion different requests, the world would be in chaos. Sunny gained the insight from her teacher that God is Divine Mind. Mind is Principle, and Principle decides what prayers to answer and not to answer according to spiritual laws of harmony. Finally, Sunny had a satisfying answer to her nagging childhood question.

ORAL ROBERTS

While cleaning a lady's house, Sunny heard Oral Roberts over the radio. He gave a testimony of his spiritual healing and his praying for enough money to open up a university where any young man or woman in the world could get an education with a Christian emphasis.

Sunny said, "There's a man working for God. I'm going to help him."

The lady gave Sunny a radio to keep. Sunny tuned in Oral Roberts whenever she could. During Oral Robert's childhood and as a young man, he was sick. He also had difficulty talking because he stuttered. He promised God that, if He healed him, he'd work for God the rest of his life. Oral was healed in a short time.

Rev. Oral Roberts was proud of his Oklahoma and Indian heritage. One evening Oral Roberts was out driving with his family looking at Oklahoma land. God spoke to him, "You can have that land."

He promised, "God, if you make it possible, I'll build a school there."

Brochures were sent to Sunny about the land. There was a picture of Oral Roberts with a big wide hat on and a mule plowing the land. Sunny went to a woman practitioner from her church and asked, "Would it be all right if I sent this man money."

She said, "Yes, if it is God's work and you are led to help him, go ahead and help him. Giving doesn't keep you from being a Christian Scientist."

With all her expenses and tithes, Sunny sent Oral Roberts money. She started out sending two dollars, then three dollars, then five dollars until she had sent Oral Roberts over five hundred dollars. God helped him with other contributors, too. When the auditorium and a few other buildings were finished, Oral Roberts invited Sunny and others who had helped him to come out to Tulsa, Oklahoma, and see the university. Sunny only had to pay her way there. The Oral Roberts people provided Sunny with food and a place to stay.

The welcoming committee met Sunny at the airplane. She stayed four days and three nights. They showed her the new campus. Sunny especially liked the Grand Tower. Sunny had a wonderful time and continued to help him until the church started building the Christian Science Center World Headquarters in Boston. In one year she sent $700 to Boston for the Center. Once in a while she'd send $5 to Oral Roberts because he prayed for her. She felt the Lord had wonderfully blessed her with the power to give generously.

HELP FOR THE INDIANS

Sunny helped many people. For example, Sunny had a rummage sale for the Indians. The Indians sent her letters telling about the children who needed help. They sent pictures of children sitting on the ground with no clothes on. The pictures had stickers with your return address that you put on letters. Sunny mailed the Indians boxes of clothes. The people Sunny worked for gave her the clothes to mail. Sunny had so many bundles of clothes that she did not know what to do.

When people asked for money, she said, "Lord, what can I do? I have lots of clothes and other stuff people have given me."

The Spirit told her to have a rummage sale. She went to her white neighbors. She showed them the pictures and said she was going to have a rummage sale. They gave Sunny a multitude of different things. She opened up her garage. In two days she made $400. The Indian folks sent Sunny many letters of thanks.

THE VOICE

In the 1960's Sunny was walking to church on a Sunday morning. A thought came to her, "Pray for all fifty states." Sunny paid no attention to the voice. No one was attacking the United States of America. In the days that followed, she continued to hear in her head, "Pray for all fifty states." She ignored the voice. After hearing the voice for about a week, she thought if she prayed the voice would go away. She didn't pray.

When she read in the newspaper that the government was rewarding unwed mothers with apartments and money depending on the number of children they produced, Sunny realized why the Spirit was directing her to pray. There was an invisible force intent on destroying America. Sunny wondered what craziness and chaos the future would be for the welfare of the United States. She recalled that someone had said the only way our country could be destroyed was from within. She felt this destruction would happen when unwed girls get paid money for having children. The Spirit was telling her to be alert and pray.

From then on, Sunny prayed for blessings for her country. She felt God was guiding her to do the good God had for her to do each day. Sunny dwelled on that part of the Lord's Prayer that says, "Thy will be done in earth as it is in Heaven." She knew that just as God is governing in Heaven so is God governing on

Earth. Sunny remembered a preacher at the Saint's Church saying, "You can't have God's will on earth when you have the unwed kind of birth."

JOHN HAGGI

Sunny helped another one of God's men, Rev. John Haggi, of Atlanta, Georgia at the time. He does good work spreading God's love over the globe in India, Japan, and Indonesia. Sunny had a friend whose son, during his summers played in the band at the Grand Hotel on Mackinack Island in Michigan. This friend was going to visit her son and invited Sunny to go on the vacation with her. John Haggi was on the island speaking to a convention held at the Grand Hotel. Sunny was delighted to go and hear Rev. Haggi speak.

Rev. Haggi founded the Haggi Institute in 1969. Haggi Institute was founded and is operated to meet the need of non-western Christian leaders for excellence in leadership. It was to equip Asian, African and Latin American leaders to return to their Third World countries and train others for leadership in spreading the gospel of Christ. Their purpose was to reach their own people. The Haggi Institute has facilitated the training of Christian leaders in about 140 nations and in every Islamic nation.

The training program is headquartered in Singapore, a neutral hub of the developing world. The world is changing. Today millions of people live in countries that either bureaucratically discourage or openly prohibit foreign missionary work. John Haggi adapted his communication of the gospel to the trainees' own cultural environment.

LITTLE CITY

Little City is a community for mentally challenged children. Sunny received a brochure from Little City which is forty-five minutes west of Wilmette. It's an alternative to children living in an institution. The hope of Little City is to help mentally challenged children to lead productive lives with some dignity.

The directors were asking for donations so the children had something to do. Sunny sent $8. It was enough to buy four chickens, a rooster, and a hen for the farm.

BUDDY TUCKER

Sunny sent money to the blind folks, too. She heard Buddy Tucker testify how he'd been blind for eighteen years. God healed him, so he took up the work of preaching and broadcasting over the radio. She sent him $2 for his testimony. Whenever she could, she sent more.

Sunny said, "If you open up your heart to God, good will come in and help you give. When I send money out to help, someone calls me to do work for them, and I make the money back. Christian Science teaches, that is the way God's law of supply and demand operates. You give and then you get it back.

PRUDENCE RESULTS IN REWARDS

Some of Sunny's old customers still called her when she was in her eighties to serve and wash the dishes. She'd say, "I'll do it, if you can put up with my slowness from old age." With the money she made, she was able to pay $487 for a stove. She put the stove on the third floor to keep her roomer warm. She felt that if your renters are nice people and you make them comfortable, they will stay with you.

Sunny prepared for the future. Whatever money Sunny invests, she gets back. She kept enough money in the Federal Bank to cover expenses if she should pass on. She had a lot paid for in the cemetery. Her mama and husband were there. She bought an extra grave. In her will, Sunny left any money, after the bills were paid, to be divided among the many charities she contributed to.

In 1976 Sunny sold her home in Wilmette. Her cousin in Chicago took care of the paper work. He's a saved man. His children are Chicago school teachers and lawyers. His wife is God's woman, a good wife and mother. From then on, he took care of her financial affairs.

Because Sunny lived in Wilmette for forty-five years, she was able to live in the local apartments which the government built. The apartments are called Gates Manor. Tenants pay different amounts according to their income. Sunny was surprised to discover that she used to clean the houses of some of the tenants. Her former employers visited Sunny. They looked after each other.

Sunny took her *World Books* with her to Gates Manor. She followed the space program. She learned all big things are made up of small things. She liked to show friends her scrap book on the progress of man in space.

Sunny was living at Gates Manor on Wilmette Avenue when her doorbell rang. She answered to a man who said he was a reporter. He wanted to interview her about living in a white village like Wilmette. Sunny gave him permission to come up to her apartment. Two black reporters appeared. They asked her for specific instances when she had been mistreated by the white community.

The reporters stated, "You have lived in this all white village for many years. We know you are the only black person living here at Gates Manor."

Sunny said, "The white people on the North Shore have been good to me. They have given me extra money when I have been in need. When I had my nursery, if parents used swear words, I corrected them. They have given me gifts. No white person has said an unkind word. It's my own black people who have said unkind things about me. They have cheated me and taken advantage of me. Everything I have is because some white family gave me work. No colored family ever gave me a nickel."

"Could you give me an example?" one of the reporters asked.

"The radio commentator, Mr. Mel BelAires," Sunny replied. "His children are among those that I helped raise. Mel BelAires remembers me on Mother's Day and Christmas. Mr. BelAires doesn't send the flowers and check by messenger. He comes himself and visits. When he needs cheering up, he tells me I always make him feel better. I have lots of friends like that who are white and like to visit with me"

The reporter asked, "To what do you attribute you're getting along with the residents of Wilmette?"

Sunny answered, "I'd say that white people here have a bit of respect for me, and I reflect that respect back to them. The Bible teaches respect and love. So many people don't understand the Bible. I've studied it all my life. The Spirit has revealed to me the meaning."

Then the reporter asked, "Mrs. Buchanan, I'm looking for examples of white people treating you poorly."

Sunny responded, "No, Sir, I've had black people take advantage of me, steal from me and make life miserable for me in my own house. I'm sorry that I can't say anything bad against the white people in this town. Anyway, the color of your skin shouldn't make a difference. God loves all colors and is pouring out His blessings if you are listening to His blessings."

The men reporters were disappointed, said goodbye, and the two men left.

HARDEST DECISION

A woman Sunny worked for came for a visit. Sunny told her, "I want to tell you about one of the hardest things I did in my life." She told her when she was first living in her home in Wilmette, a cousin, his wife and sixteen year old son came up from Mississippi to visit. The sixteen year old son was to work on a project for school which entailed gathering specific articles in magazines and newspapers. The boy gathered the articles and put them in a huge bag. His mother told him to cut the articles out, as the bag would not fit in the car for the drive home. The boy would not cut the articles out, but insisted he was taking the huge bag with him.

The day the family left, the mother told her son he was not going the long way to Mississippi with that bag of paper. He thought he'd get his way. As the car was piled high with supplies Sunny had given them, there was scarcely room in the car for the son. Sunny watched the boy stand by the car with his bag while his parents drove away. The expression on his face was one of disbelief that he had not gotten his way.

When his parents had driven about fifty miles, they phoned to see how their son was. Sunny told them he couldn't believe they'd leave him behind, but to keep going. She'd handle it.

Sunny instructed the boy about the commandment to obey your father and mother. She told him your parents feed you, cloth you, and take care of you. If they asked you to do something wrong, you wouldn't obey, but they asked you to do a right thing, to reduce the size of the bag of paper. Now how are you going to get back to Mississippi?"

He asked Sunny to loan him the money for bus fare. Sunny prayed to God for the strength to do what was right. She told the boy he could stay with her. She would feed him, but she would not give him the bus fare because he disobeyed his parents. She said, "I'll tell you what I'll do."

She pulled out the lawn mower and a can of gasoline. She told him she'd pay him for cleaning her yard, and then he could go to the neighbors and mow their lawns until he had the bus money. Sunny prayed to do God's will in this situation. The easy thing for her to do was give him the bus money.

When the boy had enough money for the bus fare, Sunny gave him twenty-five dollars for food and emergencies to help him on his way. Sunny took him to the bus station in Chicago. She saw he got on the correct bus. When the bus pulled away, Sunny felt the deep meaning of the Saxon "Goodbye" which is "God bless you."

The boy left with his *small folder of clipped articles.* When he arrived home, his mother said he was a changed boy. In fact, that

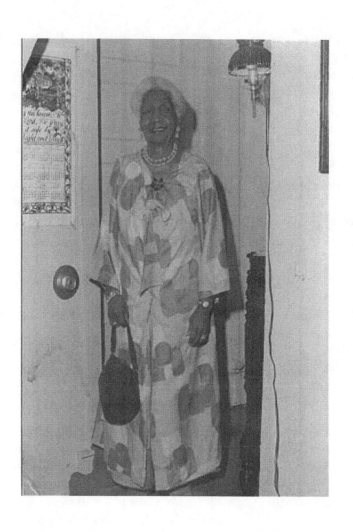

boy grew up to be a judge. He is a contributor to good in the world. It really tore Sunny's heart out to watch him struggle. She did make the right decision even though it hurt her. After all, God promised a rough time in His commandment for people who don't obey their parents.

GRATITUDE

Sunny had a humbling moment thinking back about her two sisters not taking instructions well. She recalled a disastrous learning experience where she didn't follow instructions well herself. She worked for a family in Glencoe, a North Shore suburb near Wilmette. The lady called and asked her to fix dinner for six people. She said, "Pick up whatever groceries you make best at Treasure Island but no pork." Sunny fixed her favorite foods—a roast, fresh asparagus, mashed potatoes, a salad, and cherry pie.

When the family came in the dining room, they cried and yelled that Sunny had desecrated their home. The father took the pork roast and threw it outside in the garbage. He told Sunny to leave immediately. They were orthodox Jews. It took a lot of praying for Sunny to regain her peace. Sunny realized she had a part in the blame.

Sunny said, "I'm grateful the Lord is my alarm clock. He wakes me up in the morning. I come to this window and bless and pray for everybody that walks on these streets. Next I pray for things going on in the world. My church teaches to write a list from reading the news stories in the *Christian Science Monitor*. Then I know what things to pray for in the world.

"We have a wonderful God to obey. I love everybody. Nothing against nobody. Nobody! Darling, just put it in the hands of the Father. I declare you can't beat Him. What God can't do no one else can do. All things are possible to them that believe. And I believe!" Sunny practiced the saying, "Plow deep while sluggards sleep, and you'll have corn to sell and keep."

Sunny reminisced about her husband. She wondered what she could have done to change Buck. She did feel that Buck deceived her when they got married. When Sunny married Buck, he acted like he was a saved man. After marriage, Sunny painfully discovered Buck was not the saved man he said he was. He had women, ran around with a bad crowd, bootlegged, and to make her life worse, rarely contributed money to the household. He refused to do work around the house. Sunny reluctantly concluded you can't change anybody.

She felt hurt that her mother preferred her daughters, Mattie, Bertie, and Fredona that she had with old Mr. Potts over her. Sunny was the daughter Em had with Levy. Although Em lived with her daughters on the South Side of Chicago, Sunny never gave up trying to get her mother to live with her in Wilmette. Sunny wanted her mother to like white people and black people. Sunny failed. When Sunny said something good about white people, her mother wouldn't listen. Em would praise the black people and say bad things about white folks. When Sunny explained that God loved both black and white people, Em would say, "I'm not God. I only like black people. I don't want to be in Wilmette and see white people. I only want to see Negroes." Sunny gave her mother money for her bills until the day her mother died. She had her buried near Wilmette so she could put flowers on her grave. She owned a plot big enough for Buck, her mother, and herself.

One day in autumn, Sunny stood by the fourth floor window of her apartment looking at the whole world with the eyes of a friend. She prayed for God to bless plants, people, and all things that have breath.

> Dear God, help each one in the world to understand we are brothers and sisters of the one, same God.
>
> Help us to respect and love one another.

Sunny recited a statement she studied of Mrs. Eddy's about healing prejudice:

> One infinite God, good, unifies men and nations; constitutes the brotherhood of man; ends wars; fulfills

the Scripture, "Love thy neighbor as thyself;" annihilates pagan and Christian idolatry,—whatever is wrong in social, civil, criminal, political, and religious codes; equalizes the sexes; annuls the curse on man, and leaves nothing that can sin, suffer, be punished or destroyed. (*Science and Health, p. 340*)

That Autumn day Nelson Booth's lawyer, Larry Reynolds, came into the room. Sunny sat down in her favorite chair. Larry told her that Nelson Booth had passed on. Nelson left Sunny his entire fortune knowing Sunny would know best what to do with it.

From deep in her heart Sunny said, "Thank you, dear God. Now I can put more than a *nickel in the collection.*"

Sunny spent many happy days deciding where the money would do the most good.

At 96 years, Sunny Buchanan closed her eyes to this world and opened them in the next.

> This world is not conclusion:
> A sequel stands beyond,
> Invisible, as music;
> But positive, as sound.

Emily Dickinson

A FRIEND'S RECOLLECTION

Georgia Dearborn, a friend of Sunny's, who she knew as Ammie, sent me the following to include in *Living In The Light*.

Our family was first acquainted with Ammie Buchanan in the 1960s. When our youngest son (of 6 boys) was born, she called him Timothy the Sixth, (Timothy VI).

We often included her at our holiday's meals. She once shared her table with all of us—a wonderful chicken dinner—which was a rare occasion for us. NO one invites a family of 8 for dinner! Ever!

Every few months she would call me in the morning, requesting a ride to the National Food Store on Central Avenue. The first time it turned out to be a three-hour foray, that also included bill paying at the Town Hall, shoe repair, and a long visit to the dimestore.

I loved helping her, but soon developed a scheme to shorten the food shopping. The first time took so long because she turned it into a social occasion, discussing everything about brand choices, sizes, quality, and best buys. That's how a half-hour trip was stretched into two hours.

Arriving at the Water Department, she laid her bill on the counter, bent way over, and for some minutes, fished in her clothing for something. Then she straightened up and placed several paper dollars before the cashier, and her water bill was paid and properly stamped. Later she told me that she never kept paper money in her purse. She simply folded it neatly in a clean white handkerchief, and pinned it inside her bra with a huge safety pin. She requested that if I were ever to hear that she was in a street accident, I was to rush to her and get the money out of the "First National Bank", the name she laughingly gave this unique hiding place. She didn't want the coroner to find it!

One morning she called and asked me to drive her to the cemetery where she had reserved and paid for her burial plot. We drove west of Wilmette and out Willow Road, just beyond the Glenview Air Base. We turned south a road that led to a cemetery of black folks. It was a nice, well-kept area, with no headstones, just flat name markers in the lawn, some with color photos of the decedents. It was interesting to see those faces smiling up from the grass. Soon Ammie found her "location", and we returned home.

Every moment spent with her was a rare privilege. There seemed to be no end to the love she had to share with everyone. Wise to the ways of the world, her life was a triumph of her religious spirit.

CHAPTER TWENTY

AFTERTHOUGHT

"There is a natural aristocracy in our country
the grounds of which are virtue and talent."
Thomas Jefferson

"A great thought is a great boon, for which God is to be
first thanked, then he who is the first to utter it, and then,
in a lesser, but still in a considerable degree, the man who
is the first to quote it to us."
Bovee

"The tissue of life to be
We weave with colors all our own,
And in the field of Destiny
We reap as we have sown."
John Greenleaf Whittier

A PRAYER FOR
THE WORLD

God, Divine Love, flow through each of us to bless mankind. May peace, prosperity, and brotherhood of all peoples and nations be the reality. May the oppression of the weak cease. May the reality of freedom for each man and woman educate our enemies.

Dear Father, may divine Love shield the innocent children from predators. Divine Love flows everywhere uncovering the guilty, establishing the reign of honesty, peace, and purity in our consciousness, and removing all that is unlike Love. May turmoil cease and Love flow to the glory of our Father God, who is Good. Amen

A Butterfly Blessing

Lord,

Bless me with the ability of a butterfly to endure the changes that will happen to me in my lifetime. Help me to accept these changes with a positive and loving attitude.

Bless me with the beauty of a butterfly to allow me to reflect the colors of my soul, being and individuality, and to look for these things in others.

Bless me with the ability of a butterfly to create and instill the feeling of wonder, passion, and excitement towards all of your living creatures.

Bless me with the butterflies' ability to pollinate your flowers, so that I may cultivate your human garden with love and compassion.

Last, but not least, Lord, Bless me with the grace of ascension, so that I may ascend into your glorious heaven like a rising butterfly, when my journey here on earth, is complete.

Amen

Author—M. Dilts

INDEX